CHRISTIANITY'S
SURPRISE

C. KAVIN ROWE

CHRISTIANITY'S SURPRISE

A Sure and Certain Hope

Abingdon Press

Nashville

CHRISTIANITY'S SURPRISE:
A Sure and Certain Hope

Copyright © 2020 by Abingdon Press

ISBN 978-1-7910-0820-8
LCCN: 2020944975

Scripture quotations have been translated from the original languages by the author.

20 21 22 23 24 25 26 27 28 29—10 9 8 7 6 5 4 3 2 1
MANUFACTURED IN THE UNITED STATES OF AMERICA

For Gabrielle in sure and certain hope–
and for Isaac, as always

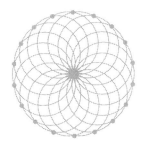

CONTENTS

ACKNOWLEDGMENTS

I would particularly like to thank the Issachar Fund for the generous support and intellectual stimulation that it provided: course relief for research and funding for numerous dinners for colleagues across various disciplines to discuss Christianity's surprise: theology, medicine, classics, literature, history, and so forth. Kurt Berends and Sara Hohnstein were not only encouraging and patient, they were also exceedingly kind. In addition, I would like to thank all of my Duke colleagues and other visitors who invested in the discussions over dinner. The conversations were invaluable to me on many different levels, not the least of which was the nurturing of collegiality and development of new friendships.

Christianity's Surprise was originally intended to be a long scholarly book, but the exigencies of life required me to rethink its form for the present. The research is there between the lines, as it were, for those who care to pursue it, but the driving vision and argument will, I hope, appeal to many well beyond my fellow scholars. If Christianity is anything at all like what the early sources claim it is, then woe to us if we forget its power, make it boring, and lose its surprise. Human life is just too hard to have a boring Christianity. My hope is that remembering some of its animating convictions and practices will surprise us all, especially now as we need hope as much as we ever have in the 21st century.

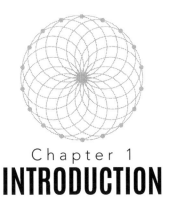

Chapter 1
INTRODUCTION

We think we already know what Christianity is. And, to some extent, we are right. On the long march from its origins until now, Christianity has penetrated almost every layer of every society and culture in the North Atlantic West. Pull out Christianity from the complex tapestry of Western history, and the whole thing would unravel. Whether in fine art or architecture, pop culture or celebrity athletes, corner churches or political debates, intellectual circles or policy wonks, Christian language, Christian images, Christian influence, and Christian legacies abound. Even the religion-haters, as misinformed as so many of them are, turn out to have Christianity in particular in mind when they go on the attack.

But in an equally important sense we are wrong. We don't really know what Christianity is. The stronger currents of the last two or three centuries have carried us away from basic Christian understandings of the human being and the world in which we live, as well as from habits of being informed by Christianity's long history that structured much of common life. The biblical God is no longer the horizon of human life; the human is an autonomous individual now, able to determine for itself what it wants for itself and how to get it; the public square is consistently championed as a place where religious people should not bring their convictions; major moral decisions are made by reference to personal preference and sentiment; churches are seen to be the same thing as other "voluntary societies"; economic realities have erased Sunday as a unique mark of the week,

1

and so on. These currents are all related in complicated ways, but the effect of their combination on present existence is rather simple to name and easy to see: we have developed societal amnesia and ignorance of what Christianity originally was—and what it still can be.

And this is the mark of our time in the West: Christianity is still so much here with us that it is utterly familiar *and* has receded from us so far that we do not know what it is. This is not a step-wise process—here, then not here—but a simultaneous reality. Christianity is at one and the same time here and gone, familiar and forgotten. This is the world in which we live.[1]

This larger environment is so pervasive, in fact, that even large swaths of Christian life itself have begun to mirror the current situation. We continue to talk of God, of course, but within an assumed framework about "justice" or "evangelism"—and many other things besides—that actually treats God as something like an important addition to the truth of specific causes people already support. We are at home and comfortable in Christian language and use it for whatever we care about, but all the while we remain strangers to the vital biblical and ecclesial patterns that originally surprised the world. We go about our work speaking Christian, as it were, but remain captive to the cultural terms that have been dictated to us.

Many Christians today thus cut off the chance for surprise and renewal in our time with an assumption that we already know what the biblical God is or should be doing in the world. Under the supposition that we already know what we need to know, we fail to develop a scriptural imagination and to learn the vibrant streams of tradition that create Christian expectation and new work—and we thus miss the revitalizing potential of rediscovery.

❊❊❊❊❊

Originally, Christianity was a surprise. It was not anticipated, and many of the things it brought with it as it came into the world were completely surprising. No one could yet take it for granted, and no one had forgotten what it was. Some—notably the Romans, off and on—did try to extinguish it, but to no avail. Instead, over the course of a few centuries,

2

Christianity grew from a minute Jewish sect into the dominant religious force in the Roman world. Sociologists of religion have various explanations for this growth—some more, some less plausible—but what should be common to all of them is the fact that no one could have predicted it.

Of course, today it seems self-evident and even rather natural to think that Christianity focuses on Jesus. He is, after all, the reason for Christianity. But we have forgotten just how radical and unheard of this was. In fact, no matter how you cut it, the most surprising thing of all about early Christianity was the unique and utterly intense focus on a singular Jew, Jesus of Nazareth.

The consequences of this focus were far-reaching, complicated, and historically explosive. There are many ways to explore these consequences, but for the sake of getting at what was and still is surprising about concentrating so intensely upon Jesus of Nazareth, we need a framework. We can get one by focusing on three central aspects of earliest Christianity that can help us to think the surprise that Christianity was and still can be: *the story of everything*, *the human*, and *institutions*. Each following chapter will discuss one of these central aspects and illuminate its surprising nature. At the same time, however, the chapters should be seen together as one picture. The story of everything, the human, and institutions are inseparably interconnected and depend on each to make sense of the others.

❧❧❧❧❧

At its origins, Christianity's surprise was a person, Jesus the Messiah, crucified and raised. To receive this surprise and rebroadcast it, the earliest Christians discovered that they had to tell the story of everything. And the story they told put them in the world in a particular way: Christians know they live in the time where they serve Jesus in a still-fallen world that is being newly created even now, awaits his final return, and hopes for the eternal healing of all that is. What did it mean to live in this kind of time?

At the heart of Christian discernment about this question and at the center of their surprise for the world was the revelation of the human as the image of Christ. This vision of the human—one and all—was a Christian invention and put into the world a creature that the world had yet to see. Before the Christians no one had thought that every human—whether high, low, or anything in-between—was exactly the same as every other, and no one had thought that all of them were to be treated as if they were the very Lord of the world. In a very real sense, the Christians took the human as such, and therefore each and every instance thereof, to be the "incarnation" of Jesus Christ. It is patently obvious that this vision took some time to develop, and it is patently obvious that Christians both then and now have betrayed their own vision. But that it came into the world *at all*, that it served as the compass for Christian behavior far and wide, that it made its way around the Mediterranean in a society that had no use for it—and longed for it all the same—is itself nothing short of absolutely stunning. Except perhaps for a few adumbrations from Jewish tradition, the Roman world was completely unprepared for it, and was caught by surprise.

The earliest Christians knew that to make the truth of Jesus and his image known to the world they had to do more than just announce its arrival. They needed to create ways of seeing and being that had not yet existed. So they established communities and institutions that took up space in public and made explicit through their order, structure, and practices what the human was in light of Christ. Over time the poor and the sick, for example, entered the world as new categories of people. The Roman world knew of poor people and sick people, of course, but it had never seen the "poor" as a distinct group of vulnerable people that required response, and it did not know what it was to care for the sick during a plague in spite of the risk to oneself. The Christians, however, had learned through the story of everything that they were not to fear death, that they were to see Christ in the face of the poor and the sick, and that they were to be present to them and provide for them, come what may. The sharing of resources—first among other fellow Christians, and then beyond—nursing and doctoring during the plagues, the invention of the hospital and shelters for the poor. These were all Christian surprises for the world.

So, too, were the Christian political and educational stances, which were intrinsically necessary for the rapid growth and staying power of early Christianity. Already by the late first and early second century, the

Christians surprised the world overtly by their refusal to worship any of the gods high or low, including the Roman Emperor, and by their refusal of basic daily patterns of pagan life such as feasts and festivals. The Romans knew the Jews were an ancient people and thus gave them some leeway for their unique practices, but in the eyes of the Romans the Christians were not (or not quite) Jews and were thus perplexing, surprising—and obstinate. Their reasonableness could not be counted on, and when they came too much into the public eye, they needed to be punished. The way the Christians bore punishment and martyrdom was also surprising. Like their Lord, the Christians refused to worship that which they should not and went willingly to their deaths in the confidence of eternal life.

Their education was less visible at first but no less remarkable. Not only did they teach what Jesus taught them and cultivate the memory of him and of the early days of the church, they also aimed to replace the foundational texts that typically formed the Roman educated imagination with Christian scripture. Their point was not that there was nothing worth learning in the pagan world. Much to the contrary, their point was that to be in the world as they were called to be in the world they had to relate everything else to the truth elaborated in scripture. When they studied Greek philosophy at Origen's university in Caesarea, for example, they studied it within a wider Christian way of being that united their intellects with the Christian practices that they took to be derived from scripture. Their tie to the biblical text was thus a tie to the wellspring that repeatedly funded and nourished the surprise in action.

✸✸✸✸✸

To be sure, the Christians were not thinking explicitly about how to be surprising or focusing on a particular method that generated surprise as a way to grab attention, make headlines, and allow them to make their case. They were instead engaged with a different set of fundamental questions that were internal to their lives as Christians. How can we be Christians? In light of our story, what reigning stories do we need to challenge? In light of our vision of the human, what do we need to be doing that's not being done? In light of the need to learn and remember who we are, what do we need to teach, and what do we need to learn?

For the earliest Christians, that is, the surprise for the world was a natural outgrowth of their comprehensive and integrated way of being. It is because the Christians discovered their place in the story of everything, for example, that they were able to say what the human is in light of Christ; and it is because of their vision of the human that they developed institutions that taught and showed what it was. But it was also by teaching and showing what the human was that the story of everything was interpreted in real time/space for the world to see; and it was the human from the story of everything that the institutions most vividly depicted. Proclaiming Jesus as the crucified and risen Lord of the world, saying no to the emperor and gods, nursing the plague-ridden and founding an orphanage, teaching and interpreting scripture, setting up offices of bishop and deacon—all these things, and more, were not so much individual works of early Christianity as they were the single creative work that was required by integrated Christian life. To be in the world as Christians was to do all these things at once.

Christianity's surprise thus went out in many directions simultaneously. For the early Christians, to put it simply, the surprise for the world was the same thing as being Christian in the first place.

I believe that we need to be asking the same fundamental questions as were the early Christians. My contention is that asking them with some knowledge of how Christianity was originally surprising will help us to ask them better today and to rediscover the surprising power of Christianity in our midst. There is obviously not a one-size-fits-all answer to the questions, but Christians today in the West are hungry for a revitalization of our imaginations and practices that show the world who we are and why we exist.

And the world itself is hungry for authentic witness to truth. The eruption of social media and the accompanying information explosion has brought many goods but it has also left the world in a state of perpetual disarray. With so many options on offer, with so many claims to our attention, and with so many around-the-clock contenders for "how things really are" the overall environment is a buzzing ball of confusion. The world knows not where it is headed. And it thus thrashes about in memories of what was lost when it left Christianity behind and struggles aimlessly to make some moral order out of the current chaos.

We Christians have plenty of terrible press and humiliating moral disgrace, and though the view of the human told by the story of everything should lead us to expect our own repeated failure, the sheer volume of the problems can too easily overwhelm our sense of what we have to stand on and what we have to offer. But if we are ultimately the same people as the early Christians and stand in the same tradition with them—and we are and do—then we should expect to be surprised by what we have to offer and to surprise the world with it.

Of course, there are vast differences between Christian life in the first couple of centuries and today. We cannot simply reinstate the exact kind of things the early Christians started as if twenty centuries have not gone by with their multilayered, immensely complicated cultural and ecclesial differences. We can, however, learn from the early Christians how to foster and renew the imagination required to develop fruitful witness and work. The surprise of Christianity for today, that is, is not a simple "now go and do this" five-year program. It is, instead, a call to a patient discernment of the heart of Christian witness in a complex world of "here and gone" where familiarity, ignorance, distortion, opposition, disappearance, and love of things Christian simultaneously occur.

Such complexity means that what it is to be Christian in the West is up for grabs. It is "up for grabs" because our present moment is so confusing, so misleading, and so promising all at once. Christianity will always be intertwined with the cultures in which it comes to exist; there is no such thing as uninculturated Christianity. But our current inculturation teaches us by habit and media exposure to think we have seen genuine Christianity on constant display, when in fact what we often see are only its various extremes or distortions. For example, one minute we hear a megapreacher claiming that God is finally bringing America back to its

Christian roots; the next we read about the president of a famous seminary who denies the resurrection of Jesus. The very next we hear about the impending "rapture"; and directly after that we're told that Christians are supposed to achieve nothing less than full justice in this present world. We also know, of course, about Christianity's precipitous decline in once-thriving communities: the mainline denominations in America are clearly drying up and withering. And the Roman Catholics and the Southern Baptists have been beset by scandals. Taken together, all of this cries out for a fresh voice and a fresh vision, in short, for the surprise that Christianity brings.

Reinvigorating present Christian witness will not, however, be easy; it will require us both to engage in deep and habitual formation in the core patterns of the tradition and to create communities of discernment and risk charting some new paths. And doing these things, to put it plainly, will take time. The work of recovering the surprise of the early tradition and embodying it today cannot avoid taking time. There is no way magically to stop Christians from playing seesaw politics—crying "God's back in charge" or "the rapture's coming," depending on who's in control at the moment—or to convince various ideologically driven groups overnight that there are more important things than one's self-proclaimed identity or desires for this-worldly political change. To the contrary, the work of training Christians in the fundamentals of what made Christianity so explosively powerful when it entered the world will demand diligent and prolonged effort in both formal and informal ways: grade schools, seminaries, divinity schools, colleges, universities, churches, parachurches, coalitions, community centers, youth sports, local clubs, various media outlets, online/distance learning, faith-based social services and innovation, foundations, philanthropies, redemptive entrepreneurship, and more. In brief, we need to be nimble and boldly pursue fresh ways of educating, forming partnerships, and living out the truth of the gospel. We should not expect our effort to reweave the tattered social fabric if by that we have in mind a return to some version of a nominally Christian society of earlier decades. Such times are long gone. But we can expect, as the early Christians did, to see God at work in startling and palpable ways in the full range of how people actually live in the world. And we can turn our imaginations loose in service to God's good work.

Ours is a time where reaching to the wellspring of the tradition and responding creatively might well be the wisest and best way to reintroduce authentic Christian witness in the midst of the confusion and clamor. Surprise, in fact, is baked into the very stuff of Christian origins. Focusing on it takes us into the heart of what it is to understand Christianity at all, and thus what it is to remember and relearn the life-giving power and witness that went with being Christian at the beginning. This remembering and relearning can, in turn, surprise us all over again and chart a life-giving and hope-filled course for our witness today.

Chapter 2
THE STORY OF EVERYTHING

Novelist Barbara Hardy once wrote that "we dream in narrative, day-dream in narrative, remember, anticipate, hope, despair, believe, doubt, plan, revise, criticize, construct, gossip, learn, hate and love by narrative."[1] Her point was not that narrative is important. She takes that for granted. Her point is much more significant: narrative is the stuff within which our whole lives are lived.

Which means that we live by stories.

The *story of everything* is a story about all there is. The very earliest Christians believed that the God who elected Abraham and his offspring and who raised Jesus of Nazareth from the dead was the one who made all that is not God. There is God and not-God, and that is all there is.

When, therefore, you tell a story about that God you are telling a story about everything.

The scope of this story cannot be overestimated. It really is *everything*. Think, for example, about the difference between the story of God and all that is not-God and the "Big Bang" theory. The Big Bang is not a story about all there is. It is the best theory on the market about why things in the known universe are arranged the way they are and how they behave given certain modes of observation. Despite much gross misunderstanding on this point, that is, the Big Bang theory is not a story of origins or a story of our end. A story of origins answers the question, Why is there something rather than nothing? This natural science cannot do. It picks up immediately after this first question and asks a second, Why do the things that are here appear/behave the way they do? The story of our end answers the question, Where are we ultimately headed and for what? This, too, natural science cannot answer. The most it can say is that the physical understanding of the universe shows that it is expanding, and that the processes included in its expansion will likely be the same in the future as they have been and are now. About our ultimate purpose or destiny in the future, it necessarily remains mute. The most comprehensive scientific theory known to us, that is, always works within the parentheses of origin and end, never outside of them. In practice many natural scientists do, of course, provide their opinions about origins and end, but when they do so they have stepped out of the role of scientist and into the role of myth-maker or priest or prophet or adherents of a religion. They speak not as proponents of a scientific theory but as simple individuals offering their personal preferences about things that in principle lie beyond scientific knowledge. The story of everything, by stark contrast, does answer the question of origins and end, and thus, as it turns out, of purpose in the present and hope for the future.

The early Christians developed the story of everything through reflection on the significance of the crucifixion and resurrection of Jesus from the dead. While no one disputes the crucifixion, some (so-called) theologians have recently denied the importance of the resurrection. They have thought that you can jettison the resurrection and keep the Christianity. This is utterly strange—and false—historically no less than theologically. Let it be clearly said: without the resurrection, there would never have been anything called Christianity. No resurrection, no Christianity. For the early Christians, the resurrection is the central truth around which all other matters turn. Indeed, for them, it is nothing less than the way God himself is identified: God is the one who raised Jesus from the dead. Take away the resurrection, they thought, and God disappears, too. God's story about himself and all that he made is a story about the way in which the resurrection of Jesus catalyzes a new understanding and a new way of being precisely because of the new reality that God brought into the world—life over death, the reversal of Eden, the hope of the future, and the power in the present.

In order to understand the central components of the story of everything, we need to explore its genesis. Getting down to the basic dynamics from the life of Jesus that informed the initial surprise for the Christians will allow us to identify and trace the impact of his resurrection on the way the Christians understood the implications of the story.

The Surprise of Crucifixion and Resurrection: The Origins of the Story of Everything

The origins of the story of everything lie in the life, death, and resurrection of Jesus. When that is forgotten, the story becomes just one more version of humanity's attempt to talk about itself with the word *God*. Focusing on Jesus, however, identifies God as the one who raised Jesus from the dead, and anchors the story in the original surprise that launched Christianity into the world. In order to see how that came about, we need first to understand the importance of the link between messianic expectation and Jesus's crucifixion.

Talk of messiahs was frequent in the ancient Jewish world around the time of the New Testament. There was a variety of expectations, hopes, and dreams that went with such talk, and no composite picture that meant "messiah."[2] What was common to messiah talk, however, was the sense that to be the Jewish Messiah was to be a political figure. What was also common to messianic expectation was an assumption about failure: if the man who might be the Messiah failed in his mission, he was, by definition, not *the Messiah*. The New Testament and the early Christian literature immediately thereafter reflect both of these beliefs about the Messiah.

When the angel Gabriel visits Mary, the future mother of the Messiah, he says that her child "will be great, and will be called the Son of the Most High; and the Lord God will give to him the throne of his father David, and he will reign over the house of Jacob forever; and of his kingdom there will be no end" (Luke 1:32-33). On the surface of it, the Messiah in Gabriel's announcement is clearly a royal figure who will reestablish the Davidic monarchy in the midst of foreign rule and who will have descendants upon descendants to rule after him, free from the domination of any outside power. Mary's Magnificat, the song she sings after learning from Gabriel about her place in God's plan and the hope of Israel, further describes messianic hope.

> My soul magnifies the Lord and my spirit rejoices in God my Savior, for he has regarded the low estate of his handmaiden; for the Powerful One has done great things for me, and holy is his name. And his mercy is on those who fear him from generation to generation. He has shown strength with his arm and scattered the proud in the thoughts of their hearts; he has pulled down the powerful from their thrones and exalted the humble; he has filled the hungry with good things, and the rich he has sent away empty. He has helped his servant Israel in remembrance of his mercy, as he spoke to our fathers, to Abraham and his posterity forever (Luke 1:46-55)

Christians have long understood Gabriel's announcement and Mary's song spiritually and reread them in light of what we know the gospel's ending is: Jesus is not here literally to take up the sword and fight against the Roman oppressors on the way to simple earthly kingship, the reclaiming of the land, and a united Israel. But within the world of Luke's story, Mary's song expresses the hopes that go with a political Messiah. In the time inside the story-world, Jesus is not even yet born. Keeping this in mind allows us to hear Mary's hopes on a more mundane level: the Messiah will come as a political figure whose work and victory will involve throwing down the foreign overlords (high), exalting the Jewish people (low), reestablishing the Davidic Monarchy, and glorifying God through the purifying of worship in the reconstituted, Jewish land.

This set of expectations follows Jesus all the way through his ministry. John the Baptist prepares the way. When the crowds wonder if John may be the Messiah, he denies it and speaks of the coming Messiah as the one who "will baptize you with the Holy Spirit and with fire. His winnowing fork is in his hand, to clear his threshing floor, and to gather the wheat into his granary, but the chaff he will burn with unquenchable fire" (Luke 3:16-17/Matt 3:11-12). In hindsight John's words get reinterpreted to fit with the ending of the story, but originally and within the world of the story, where Jesus has not yet been crucified or raised, John's language clearly betokens a messianic revolution, coming battle, and victory of the Messiah over his enemies.

Even Jesus's disciples understand him in this way. When Peter famously confesses Jesus as "the Messiah," Jesus is quick to counter the revolutionary implications of such an acclamation by pointing to his coming suffering and defeat. That is who I am, Jesus teaches, but what it means for me to be that figure is not what you typically think (Matt 16:16-28; Mark 8:29-38; Luke 9:20-27). Peter does not get the point of Jesus's reshaping of messianic expectations and ratchets up his dedication to his original sense of Jesus Messiah—suffering and defeat shall never be yours, Jesus Messiah—and earns him a stern rebuke ("get behind me, Satan"). Notable sayings such as, "If anyone wants to follow me, let him deny himself, take up his cross and follow me. For whoever would save his life will lose it; and whoever loses his life for my sake and the good news will save it" (vv. 24-25) and "Truly, I say to you, there are some standing here who will not taste death before they see that the kingdom of God has come with power" are typically spiritualized too quickly by modern readers (Mark 9:1). In the time of the Gospels' story-world, Jesus's words would have been heard as earthly political statements marking the cost of messianic upheaval and battle. And in the garden of Gethsemane, the disciples have swords not because Galilean fishermen and other common workers were in the habit of carrying swords—or even knew how to use them—but because they want to be prepared for the coming battle. When Jesus enters Jerusalem, the crowds' cries of "Blessed is he who comes in the Name of the Lord—the King!" articulate their earthly messianic hopes: the entrance into Jerusalem at Passover is the public declaration of the New King who is here to begin the revolt. The timing is perfect: thousands and thousands of pilgrims have come to Jerusalem for Passover, the annual celebration of the foundational liberation from Egypt. The Jewish people are gathered from across the lands all in one place, and they are ready for the celebration and renewal of the Exodus. And the Messiah is at hand to lead them.

And here the first real surprise occurs: rather than embrace the Messiah and organize around him to begin the work to free Israel, rather than acclaim and exalt him as the liberator from the hands of their oppressors, follow him as the hope of Israel—rather than any of this, the plot takes a drastic turn, and the Messiah is arrested and taken away.

The Jewish leadership in Jerusalem did not see Jesus as their savior but as a messianic pretender, and thus as a danger to the welfare of the people. Contrary to what the movies show, Passover was one of the only times the Roman governor and extra troops were actually in the Jewish capital itself.[3] And they were there, of course, because of the swell of population during the pilgrimage feast and the resultant rise in the risk of disorder. When disorder reached a certain level, the Romans would typically respond swiftly and decisively. A messianic movement, the Jewish leaders knew, would catalyze the people and provoke the Romans to violent repression. Jesus's question to his captors in the garden shows what the leaders were worried about: "Have you come out to me with swords and clubs as if I were a revolutionary?" The word I've translated "revolutionary" is typically translated "bandit," but that translation is too bland and does not capture the significance of Jesus's remark. The arrest is serious and specific: we will bring you by force if necessary and stop this movement before it gets out of hand.

Peter, at least, knows the moment for revolt is imminent, and thus attempts to cut the head off one of the apprehenders and begin the battle (Malchus, the slave of the High Priest).[4] To arrest the Messiah was unthinkable; the attempt must mean it is time to get it on.

But the Messianic expectations unravel still more. Jesus does not overwhelm his accusers, and they do not see clearly who he is. Instead, they capture him and then cleverly work the back channels to influence the people's perception of Jesus and help turn them against him. "Would the Messiah really get arrested? Are we not the leaders of the people? Do we not know the scriptures? Would we *not* know the Messiah? Do you want Pilate to slaughter us for the sake of a pretender?" Shifting and shaping the opinion of the crowds has nothing to do with jealousy or hatred of Jesus or anything else. It is simply political wisdom gained by years of working with the Romans. Show the Roman governor that he can quiet the people, satisfy the local leaders, and eliminate a chance for disorder, and he will gladly act. By the time Jesus has been "tried" by the Jewish high court (the Sanhedrin) and brought before Pilate, it is clear what the plan had been: they must get him to confess that he is the Messiah, which is why they ask him repeatedly and bring false witnesses for an extra measure, who allege Jesus plans for revolutionary violence ("destroy the Temple in three days"; see Matt 26:61; Mark 14:58); they will then report to Pilate Jesus's messianic "confession"; and they will then tell Pilate that of course he is but a pretender and reassure Pilate that the people will support the leadership's decision. For his part, Pilate can act on their accusations without fear of either inciting the crowds toward protest and riot or unnecessarily clashing with the local ruling authorities who help him to keep things as functional as possible on a regular basis. It is a win-win for order in Jerusalem.

The unexpressed presupposition of the entire scene is that "Messiah" means a political figure who will liberate Israel, that is, a revolutionary. Without this understanding of Messiah, nothing in the Passion narrative of the Gospels makes any real historical sense. No one is against Jesus because he is too loving or too kind or too inclusive or too theologically risky or whatever. Roman governors do not act on such matters and vastly prefer to let "strange" local religious disputes be solved by the adherents or locals themselves, as the reaction of another prominent governor in the New Testament illustrates (Gallio in Corinth, Acts 18). The worry on the Jewish side is bloodshed, Roman retaliation for disorder amounting to an uprising, and the loss of Jewish lives. (And on the Roman side, any avoidance of tumult is always advantageous for the governor and his reputation back home.) The leaders, that is, clearly understand that to be the Jewish Messiah is to have a politically explosive identity, and they take action based on their conviction that Jesus is not the Messiah. Violence in Jerusalem is thus avoided—with, of course, a rather serious exception.

Jesus's "trial" before Pontius Pilate goes horribly wrong. Pilate judges him innocent of the crime of *stasis*—fomenting riotous revolt amounting to sedition/treason—but sentences him to death anyway. The crime of *stasis* was a capital one, and the punishment for those who were not

Roman citizens was crucifixion (or being thrown to the beasts; for citizens it was beheading). Jesus was thus crucified with the other revolutionaries scheduled for execution.[5]

The crucifixion was a true spectacle, a public display of what happens to those who attempt messianic politics. Jesus is mocked not only through the superscription "King of the Jews"—Pilate's understanding of "Messiah"—but also actively by the leaders and onlookers who know what a Messiah is supposed to be able to do: "He saved others; he cannot save himself. Let the Messiah, the King of Israel, come down now from the cross, that we may see and believe" (Mark 15:32/par.).[6] As is the case with the previous events, so it is with the crucifixion: the superscription and all the taunting make sense only on the supposition that the Messiah was a figure who would do the conquering and that he was not supposed to get killed.

Jesus's closest disciples desert him and scatter not because they are spineless cowards but because their world is falling apart and almost nothing they have thought and believed is making sense. The Messiah is captured, tried, and now executed. Their messianic hopes have been dashed and destroyed. "We had hoped," say the grieving disciples on the way to Emmaus, "that he was the one to redeem—to *liberate*—Israel" (Luke 24:21). The implication is clear: but he *wasn't*. However the script was supposed to run, it was not supposed to end like this: the denunciation, defeat, and death of the Messiah.

But, a reader of the Gospels might say, didn't Jesus prepare his disciples for just this? After all, he told them at least three different times that the Messiah must "go to Jerusalem and suffer many things from the elders and chief priests and scribes, and be killed, and on the third day be raised" (Matt 16:21 passim). Why were they not ready for Jesus on "the third day"? Why didn't they show up at the tomb blasting forth on some trumpets, demonstrating their renewed enthusiasm for the Messiah and his liberation?

Whatever the disciples understood at the time of Jesus's instructions about the suffering Messiah, the logic of the unfolding story makes clear that the entire sequence of capture and crucifixion devastates their knowledge. By the time Jesus is executed, they know only that the question about who he really is has been answered by a public judgment against their original belief.

Yet, how could the disciples anticipate something that had never happened and had no historical precedent?

The surprise of rejection and crucifixion was followed by the surprise that ultimately makes Christianity what it is: the resurrection of Jesus from the dead. The resurrection of Jesus from the dead was unanticipated by the disciples in any real sense of knowing what to hope for or expect. And for good reason.

According to the New Testament, the resurrection was not simply the next step in Jesus's ongoing life as if it were an unbroken, natural sequence. In contrast to the Platonic view of the immortal soul in which the soul continues straight through death—being immortal, it cannot die—and is at last free of the imprisoning body, the resurrection was new life from the really and truly dead. The resurrection came from God's side of the Creator/creature distinction, and it was God's rejection of rejection, the defeat of execution and death, and a victory of life for the suffering Messiah. In the resurrection of Jesus, God confirmed that Jesus was in fact his Messiah (Acts 2:36)[7]—and henceforth identified himself as the God who raised Jesus from the dead.

That this confirmation of the meaning of "Messiah" was a radical deviation from the prevailing sense of the expectations is shown by the fact that the resurrected Jesus has to instruct his disciples in how to see the suffering Messiah in scripture (if it were all so clear ahead of time, they would have known where to look in scripture and what to expect). And not once, but twice. "Was it not necessary," Jesus asks the Emmaus road travelers, "that the Messiah should suffer these things [arrest, torture, crucifixion] and enter into his glory?" And then "beginning with Moses and all the prophets, he interpreted to them in all the scriptures the things concerning himself" (Luke 24:26-27). And then again for the eleven and the other disciples gathered with them in Jerusalem "he opened their minds to understand the scriptures and said to them, 'Thus it is written, that the Messiah should suffer and on the third day rise from the dead, and that repentance and forgiveness of sins should be preached in his name to all nations" (24:45-47). When you need an exegetical course from Jesus, you know that you do not know what you need to know.

Having learned from Jesus how to understand scripture's witness to the suffering and resurrected Messiah, the early Christians could in hindsight discern God's plan in all that had transpired. It was necessary that "everything written about me in the law of Moses and the prophets and the psalms must be fulfilled" (Luke 24:44). The good news of God was promised beforehand—literally, *pre*-promised—"through his prophets in the holy scriptures" (Rom 1:2). And it became possible to "argue from the scriptures" with other Jews and "explain and demonstrate that it was necessary for the Messiah to suffer and to rise from the dead" (Acts 17:2-3). But such retrospective rereading of scripture and the remarkable discoveries it prompted never replaced the basic sense that in "real time" the death and resurrection of Jesus was a complete surprise in the face of the disciples' expectations.

What the resurrection meant for the world was the unpacking of their surprise: when they thought about God's victory of life over death in conjunction with Jesus's ministry, they began to see that a new world had dawned right in their midst. Jesus's resurrection showed the future, what God intended for humanity, and that future was now present, here, and creating a new world. "New creation" became the name for what happened in Jesus's resurrection.

New Creation—with the Old—as the Time in Which We Live

New creation meant that the resurrection of Jesus reshaped the way the disciples understood reality. Jesus was the culmination of Israel's election and history—the goal and purpose of the Law, as Paul famously puts it in Romans 10:4—and he became the lens through which all things were seen and understood. Jesus stood alive with God on God's side of death and was bringing that resurrection life into the present. We are "born again to a living hope through the resurrection of Jesus Christ from the dead" (1 Pet 1:3).

As many thinkers have long observed, the Christian experience of Jesus's resurrection created a new sense of time. And that new sense of time created a new sense of how to be in the world.

Jewish tradition saw history as the outworking of their election, of course, and looked for the "world to come," but as a whole the rest of the world took the cosmos to be cyclical or steadily and unchangingly eternal. The early Christians, by contrast, thought that all of time had a narrative arc, which was disclosed through the advent, death, and resurrection of Jesus. All of time was related to this particular event—moving toward it from God's creation and from it to the consummation of all things in God's final reconciliation of the world to himself.

The nodal points of the story were the creation, the fall, the election of Israel, Jesus Christ and the church, and the consummation. Schematizing all of time in this way made it possible to locate human lives in the drama of all created life. The story of everything, that is, was not only comprehensive in scope, it also prompted the questions, What time is it? Where do we live now?

The early Christians' answer to the time of our world did not conceive of these different nodal points as rigid, block-like successive stages, as if we had moved entirely past the fall when we entered the time of Christ. To the contrary, their narrative was uniquely complicated and allowed a more dexterous answer: while on the one hand time is moving forward from creation to consummation—the "commonsense sense" we have of past, present, and future—on the other hand it is simultaneously true that we live in the time of the overlap of the ages (1 Cor 10:11). With the resurrection of Jesus, the future has arrived in the present. All things that exist are created; all things that exist have been and continue to be marred by the fall; all things that are marred by the fall are being and continue to be healed by the presence of New Creation in our midst; all things are therefore getting a foretaste of what's finally to come. The consummation reaches from the future into the still-plagued present. The story of everything thus looks not only forward but also backward. It is a retelling of all of creation from the vantage point of the end. And it claims that we can have a taste of God's good future even now in the midst of time.

The question then became, What do we do—how do we act—given that Jesus's resurrection has disclosed our time as a time of New Creation in the midst of the Old? If the story that tells about all things tells us that we live now in a fallen world being transformed, what does it say about how we should live in that time?

The early Christians' answer was nothing if not multidimensional. Precisely because it is a story of everything, that is, everything is affected, and they had to be creative. We can, however, summarize this creatively varied response to Jesus's resurrection by saying that as it is lived out, the story of everything is a story of witness and transformation—and not one without the other.

After our long exposure to Christianity, it can sometimes be easy to forget something simple about it, which is this: Christianity is most fundamentally about Jesus Christ. The earliest Christians never lost sight of this. In a world that had never heard of Jesus Christ, it was necessary to draw attention to him again and again as the reason for their existence and presence. The Christians continually announced him and tied their action to their witness to Jesus and the power of his resurrection currently at work in them. Which is to say that for the Christians for the first few centuries the answer to what do we do in the New Creation was "bear witness to Jesus Christ as the agent of this new world." Whatever the Christians had to offer the world, they thought, was dependent on the prior reality of the life-giving power of the living Jesus. There was no possibility for them that Christianity was, say, a social platform with an optional religious dimension. The story that made sense of the world was the same story that required them to confess Jesus as Lord at every twist and turn.

Confessing Jesus as Lord and witnessing to him was not, however, something different from the way the Christians tried to live as a people transformed. Once one understands that the story of everything encompasses everything, the inseparable connection between witness and transformational living is easy to see. You live according to the story that tells you how to live.

As philosopher Charles Taylor has repeatedly noted, a hallmark of modern life is the loss of the belief in human transformation. For the early

Christians, however, transformation was something like the point. The power of the resurrection meant transformation. Jesus Christ was "raised from the dead so that we, too, might walk in newness of life" (Rom 6:4). To deny the possibility of transformation would be to deny the resurrection. (It is no accident, then, that as modern people have given up on transformation, they have also given up on the resurrection of Jesus Christ. These are correlate affirmations and denials.)

Transformation was both personal and systemic. There was no division as yet between Christian piety and society. The Christians uniformly assumed that transformed behavior was a mark of being Christian, and they uniformly assumed that Christians would resist prevailing societal patterns that cut across Christian existence. There was, however, a direction in this work that is important to note: their impetus was not to change the world in the contemporary sense of bringing their "cause" to bear on specific issues. It was rather to bear witness to Christ in ways the world could see—communally and individually. They distinguished themselves specifically *as Christians,* not as social or political engineers (see esp. 1 Peter; Epistle to Diognetus; Apostolic Constitutions). That being Christian, however, positioned them in the world in ways that called for its transformation is everywhere in the pages of early Christian literature.

What the story of everything thus required at a very deep level was the unity between claiming to be disciples of Jesus Christ and behaving in accordance with this claim. Where witness and transformation come apart, both are imperiled. Living according to some "other gospel," as Paul would put it, or some other rule of life, would automatically testify to someone other than the risen Christ (e.g., Gal 1; 2 Cor 11:4). And testifying to someone other than the risen Christ would be to forgo his resurrection power and miss the chance at transformation. Put negatively, the early Christians were acutely aware of the power of hypocrisy to destroy their witness. No one likes to see Christians who talk about being Christian and live like something else. This was as true in the ancient world as it is today. Conversely, living in the transformative power of the resurrection and thereby witnessing to Jesus Christ was immensely attractive. Human lives that actually change and move toward and in patterns of healing and joy were as attractive then as they are now.

Crucifixion and Resurrection as the Pattern of the Story of Everything

Learning from the Christian narrative how to name the time we live in—our future with God has arrived through Jesus in the still-groaning world—also teaches us that Jesus's crucifixion and resurrection is the key to the pattern of the story of everything. That is to say, the story of everything makes reality "readable" in light of this pattern. The texture of the time in which we live is crucifixion and resurrection. Human existence is one of suffering and hope, of being crushed and of being resilient. Seen existentially, the crucifixion/resurrection pattern casts its light on every corner of human life; there is no place in human existence where crucifixion does not apply and no place where resurrection is not possible.

The crucifixion spoke truly about the ongoing presence of the fall and the rough grain of the world as we experience it. The Savior comes in our midst to bring the things that make for peace, but the rulers of the world see him not and crucify the Lord of Glory (1 Cor 2:8). Human life is thereby revealed in all its darkness. Not only can we not help killing each other, we will even kill the Lord who comes to heal us. The crucifixion, that is, is commentary on the truth of the human condition. Everywhere there are humans, there will be crucifixion. Suffering abounds. Relationships built on trust fracture and dissolve. Communities come apart. Leaders disappoint and fail. Peoples are enslaved. Children fall ill. Dreams crumble. Hopes are dashed. The Messiah is executed. The disciples desert him and scatter. Life loses. Death wins.

And yet.

The story of everything declares that the resurrection of Jesus discloses the finer grain of the world as a world destined for redemption and provides hope in the face of the reality of crucifixion. The early Christians knew—as many moderns do not—that were the life of Jesus of Nazareth to end in crucifixion, were there to be no resurrection, the story we would tell about him would be tragic. Crucifixion would be the deepest reality, and any hope we could muster would always be tempered by the realization that our race against decay and death would end in final defeat. All the love we could share and receive, all the good we could do and have done for us, all the striving toward betterment would amount in the end to nothing. Sentimental attempts to wring comfort out of our good feelings about our relationships or our deeds in the world would be nothing but sentiment—paltry, pathetic, self-comfort that would vaporize under the admission of the truth. Assurances that the world is getting better (as in Steven Pinker's popular analysis) would be as meaningless as they are strange. No terminal cancer patient is content knowing that someone, somewhere is getting richer. No child forced into rebel militias or gangs or trafficking is delighted with the fact that first-world conditions are improving, that the healthy are getting healthier and the comfortable more comfortable. So, too, satisfaction or pride in one's good work would always be accompanied by the realization that it can't last and that those behind you can always undo what you've done. No amount of rich marriage eases the severing of intimacy that comes with death of a spouse. All this is to say, the power of the resurrection to provide hope has nothing whatsoever to do with being positive in the face of the truth of death or fooling ourselves about our fragility and the fragility of what we love.

To the contrary, the resurrection of Jesus makes hope the foretaste of God's real victory in bringing life out of real suffering and real death. The early Christians, especially the martyrs, knew that they would suffer and die and that all worldly worth would go the way of the flesh, but they also knew that God's final word about all there is is not death but life. This knowledge emboldened them in the face of sin and suffering and helped them create and steward sites of hope—sometimes even their own bodies (Stephen, Paul, Peter, Ignatius, Polycarp, Perpetua, Felicity et al.). They spoke of their suffering as sharing in the sufferings of Christ, of being co-crucified, not because they thought suffering itself was salvific but because they understood the way of the cross to be the way to life. They shared in his sufferings knowing that they would be raised as he was. Hope, that is, is the hope that we will be raised with Christ and that whatever good comes from our obedience on this side of death is ultimately good only because we will live, as does Jesus, with God on the other side of our deaths. In short, the resurrection is the event and the language for the defeat and reversal of pain and death in crucifixion. We are crucified with Christ and will thus be raised with him. It is the joy that comes with the morning. Sinners repent. The disciples believe. The scriptures are opened. Slaves are freed. Orphans are tended. The sick are nursed. Death loses. Life wins.

Resurrection, however, does not undo the crucifixion as if it never happened, but takes it up, absorbs it, and makes something new from it. Jesus does not lose his wounds but has a new, incorruptible body. He is not simply reanimated, brought back to live in the world unchanged. Indeed, God's power at work in the resurrection of Jesus makes more out of crucifixion than was there to begin with. This is why the resurrection inaugurates re-creation, or new creation. It brings, we can say, *surplus-life.* Victims of genocidal violence not only survive, but then go on to adopt orphaned children and build schools to educate them. Gang members recover a sense of purpose, learn how to be in the world, and find they are deeply loved. Drug addicts get into recovery and flourish. Marriages falter and then recover and survive. Love is practiced. The church is born. The gospel is carried outward. Martyrs are made. The Christians keep growing. In the resurrection of Jesus, eternal life comes into the present and beckons us forward to a good future of everlasting blessing. No more pain. No more tears. Only joy.

Consequences/Effects/Implications: The Story and Other Stories

Precisely because it is comprehensive, the story of everything puts Christians in the world vis-à-vis other stories in ways that are critically important to understand. Understanding that your life is storied by the Christian narrative, that is, requires you to engage in questions about how this narrative interfaces with others. There are many and vastly complicated narratives that make up human life, and they often intertwine and coexist not only in any given culture but also in communities and individuals themselves. Whether such narratives are compatible or contradictory is the question of whether your life makes sense or is fragmented into a bundle of contradictions or of whether your community will survive through time or crumble beneath its internal incoherence. In the conclusion to this book, we will look at the most powerful counter-narrative about the human in Western life, and we will ask how it interfaces with the Christian story of everything. To learn from this interface how we should think and live today, however, we need first to understand something of the way the story of everything worked for the earliest Christians. This will give us the sense of how the narrative works in conjunction and collision with other stories.

There are three types of powerful narratives that were current when Christianity first emerged that merit comment. The first narrative is Israel's story. Despite much later polemics between Jews who did not take Jesus to be the Messiah and Christians—both Jewish and Gentile—who did, the earliest Christians were deeply engaged with Israel's scripture, Israel's history, and Israel's ongoing life within the budding Christian communities. In practice, there is a wide range of how the literature of the first two or three centuries deals with Israel's history, but apart from the Marcionite heresy and perhaps a few Gnostic groups, the general sense was crystal clear: there is a complex continuity between Israel and the community of Christians. The Christians claimed, that is, that their story was in fact the continuation of Israel's story; the Christian community was the place where Israel's story told in scripture was fulfilled. The purpose of Israel's election was exactly to be the light to the Gentiles ("Nations"), and this light was now going forth through the ingathering of the Gentiles ("Nations") to worship Israel's God alongside the Jewish people in a common life.

This continuity was complicated, however, because many non-Christian Jews did not agree that the direction of their scripture ran toward Jesus of Nazareth and his followers. The problem that vexed Paul, Luke, Justin Martyr, and others, that is, was the lack of universal Jewish acceptance of Jesus's resurrection as the validation of his identity as

Messiah and Lord. Were not the Jews the people who waited on the Messiah and who, therefore, should have seen the Messiah when he appeared?

The story of everything presupposes that this question is intrinsic to and ongoing within Christian existence. Precisely because the narrative depends antecedently upon the scriptural story of the Jews, the story of everything shares with the Jewish people a construal of scripture (Old Testament) as the basis for the existence of God's people. And precisely because the consummation of all things has not yet occurred, the contested construal of scripture is a point for our enduring unity rather than a final split. Over against any type of pagan form of life about which we know some things, Jews and Christians are people of the same book: we read together, even if our readings and embodiments thereof differ in accordance with the way we complete the story (the New Testament; the Mishnah/Talmud).

In contrast to the relationship with the story of the Jewish people, the story of everything positions Christians in conflict with other macro-interpretative stories and their claims to comprehensive understanding and being. The pagan world had essentially three types of larger narratives that were put into question by—and conflicted with—the story of everything.

The first type was a comprehensive philosophical account of the cosmos that presupposed and reinforced a way of life. In the Roman world at the time of the New Testament, the most influential philosophy of this type was by far Stoicism. (The point would hold for any comprehensive philosophical account, but Stoicism makes the best historical illustration.) Like the Christians, the Stoics eschewed a division between thought and life, and argued that to see the truth of the Stoic narrative about the cosmos required one to become a Stoic. Conversely, adopting Stoicism as a way of life would transform a person into the kind of person that could perceive and understand the truth of the Stoic story over time. You lived into the truth of the philosophy that guided you on the path of your life. Precisely because the Christian narrative also claimed to encompass everything and to require transformation in the life of its adherents, the two stories and their ways of life conflicted. It was impossible to combine them into one larger narrative, and a choice thus had to be made between them. Neither you nor your community (or "school") could at the same time live both as the Stoic story said you should and as the Christian one did: they were mutually exclusive in the life of one person and in a community of disciples.

The story of everything thus challenged narratively and existentially the philosophic traditions that purported to give human beings the purpose of their lives and the framework within which to live them. It said to them: you do not, in fact, have a story of everything but only about a part of what is—creation—and even there you go astray by divinizing what has been made in place of the Maker; in order to tell a story about everything that is, you need to come to know not just the world itself but the God who made the world. Only then will the scheme for human life be discovered and the doors open to the path of true life in the world.

The Christian encounter with sophisticated knowledge was varied and complicated, not least because at least some of the converts had immersed themselves in pagan philosophy prior to joining the Christian community. But across the board, the earliest Christians insisted that to know the truth of things was to learn the story of Jesus's resurrection as the self-revelation of the Creator of all things and that apart from this narrative, knowledge could not save. No matter how important or distinguished the pagan thinker, no matter how much the Christians may cite from their texts, the argument was always about life. Change your life, and you will know the truth. The story of everything, that is, refused any final division between thinking and living and announced that the unity of mind and practice was the way to know God and all that God made.

The second type of macro-interpretative narrative in the pagan world was implicit and presupposed rather than explicit and articulated. It was the story about the cosmos and the human place within it that formed the background to polytheism. In terms of regular patterns of life, polytheism was ubiquitous in antiquity. Intellectuals here and there argued for one supreme, immovable, unchangeable being at the top of the ladder of being, as it were, but none of their speculative considerations were linked to a desire to contest the gods and their role in daily life of the vast majority of inhabitants in the Roman world. The gods and their rule in life were unchallenged.

There was, of course, almost unimaginable variety in the way the gods were understood and in the stories that accompanied them in their local instantiations. Polytheism was not one simple thing but a range of things. What was implicit and consistent throughout the range itself, however, was the understanding that the whole fabric of the world was like *that*— that many gods and many divine-like beings and many spirits and so on existed, were active in human affairs, and were to be honored and worshipped. Some places were more attached to some gods than others, and some were more eager for new cultic additions than others, but the entire Roman world was polytheistic in every layer of its reach.

Moreover, polytheism was not simply a "belief" system. It was a life system, which is to say that contrary to many modern understandings of religious belief where the "belief" part of things is often separated from the "practice" part, ancient polytheism was woven throughout the entire fabric of life. Living your life at all as a pagan meant living it as a polytheist. Everything from small house statues or amulets worn around the ankles or neck to large civic sculptures, buildings, and festivals, to regional reputation and control was saturated with the gods. Prayers to the gods for love and health were the most common—or at least what we have the most remaining papyri of (and, well, there are some human constants). Yet such prayers were not to the same gods all the time but to a bewildering and tremendous multiplicity of gods, some of whose names we cannot now pronounce and whose identities and characteristics vanished as history rolled on. When a new god arrived, it was simply added on to the existing number and incorporated into the patterns that made for daily life. Anyone and everyone who was born and lived in the Roman world was polytheist.

What had not occurred until the Christian story collided with the assumptions of polytheism was the possibility that the whole system was false.[8] The story of everything called into question the entire way of being that was polytheism and narrated it in all its variations as the worship of creation rather than the Creator. Polytheism was not a story or set of stories that took account of everything but a multifaceted interpretation and exaltation of all that was not-God. The true God had yet to come fully into the picture in the polytheistic world. Bringing God into view as the only one to be worshipped created the conditions for a clash between rival narratives and the practices that go with them (worship/sacrifice/festivals/calendar/etc.). This clash amounted to a gradual undoing and remaking of the entire religious cloth of antiquity.

For the Christians, the gods had to go. And that meant that much of the life-pattern of polytheism had to go, too. Conversion to Christianity was thus costly and required its brothers and sisters to unlearn much of what they took for granted and to replace those things with new things that put them in the world in new ways—socially, relationally, and politically.

The third type of macro-interpretative story fits within polytheism but gained a distinctive edge during the Roman Empire: the godlike or divine nature of the Roman emperor and the cult that was devoted to his worship and honor. An ancient maxim ran: "What is a God? The One who Rules. What is a King? An Equal to God."[9] Some earlier scholars of the imperial cult have wondered about the precise meaning of "divine" in relation to the living emperor, but more recent work has grasped the heart of the matter: whatever his closest associates/colleagues/enemies thought of him personally, all across the empire it was simply assumed that worship/sacrifice was what was due the emperor. His power was what it was to be a god. The understanding of the emperor as a god, that is, subsisted in the practice of the cult itself, as well as in almost countless other ways of adulation that permeated daily life (images, statues, coins, etc.). Roman imperial theology presupposed the story that told of the world as the emperor's domain as Lord and God. Whether from the Roman perspective the emperors turned out to be relatively good or exceedingly bad mattered not. The emperor as emperor was "Lord over all," as the architrave of the Parthenon said of Nero, and thus divine.

The early Christian collision with the Roman imperial theology and practice was, on the one hand, sporadic and ad hoc. There were local persecutions and clashes (in the cities of Smyrna and Ephesus, for example, or in the province of Bithynia/Pontus), but systematic persecution on an empire-wide basis did not come until AD 251 during the reign of Decius. On the other hand, however, the collision was fundamental, total, and omnipresent. The story of everything told of only one Lord of all who could be worshipped and it required of the Christians an ultimate loyalty that superseded all other demands. The earliest Christians were not out to topple Caesar or run the empire—they could not have imagined such a thing in the first place—but any and every time someone or something was set up as a rival to the true Lord, the Christians knew that they could not play along. Caesar may be a great lord, but his claim to be Lord of all usurped the identity and rule of the Lord Jesus Christ.

The story of everything thus once again reframed a basic and extensive part of Roman life as a story about something else in the place of God: imperial theology was not a part of the story of all there is but one more version of humanity's inability to speak truly about itself without the true God. In short, the story of everything put the Christians in the world politically precisely as Christians and provoked the invention of distinctively Christian political reasoning and action. Such reasoning and action took a variety of forms as the Christian movement spread and grew, but it was crystallized most dramatically in the refusal to worship/sacrifice to the emperor and deny the Lord Jesus. Where and when such refusal became public, as it did, the Christian narrative was explicitly embodied, and martyrdom followed. "Are you a Christian?" was repeatedly answered with "Yes, I am," putting forth into plain view the hope of resurrection in the face of certain death. The story of God and all that is not-God was a story to be lived, even if such living meant dying for its truth.

Conclusion

The story of everything was born at the intersection between the long history of the God of Israel with his people and the sending of his Messiah, Jesus of Nazareth. With the advent, crucifixion, and resurrection of Jesus, the early Christians realized that they needed to extend Israel's story to include all things. The story of everything thus became a story about the God who created all things, who elected Israel after the fall, who sent his Messiah Jesus, who (re)formed his people around loyalty to Jesus, and who would one day fully complete the renewal of creation when there would be no more sin and sorrow.

This narrative gave the early Christians a way to understand the time in which they lived. God's good future for humanity had arrived in the present and beckoned us forward; the time was that of new creation in the midst of the old. The story also enabled them to interpret reality in light of Jesus's crucifixion and resurrection. Narrating the world's story involved naming humanity's suffering, recalcitrance, and evil as crucifixion—the complete opposite of God's peaceful, reconciling, and salvific work. And it involved naming humanity's inability to give up on hope as the call of the resurrection to our future in life eternal—God's refusal to accept crucifixion as the final word about the world and, instead, his act to meet the brokenness of crucifixion with the life-giving work of our salvation, the resurrection.

The story also put the early Christians in the world in a way that created a unique and complicated relationship with non-Christian Jews and that positioned them counter-culturally in relation to the dominant narratives of the wider Roman world. Joining the Christian community required a reformation in the way one understood reality and one's place within it. This reformation meant that some old ways of knowing had to go and new ones had to take their place. Life-patterns had to be changed. Many deep and powerful habits long taken for granted simply as "what you do" came under scrutiny and had to be changed, too. As the early Christians told it, such change was often nothing less than tectonic in effect, profoundly difficult, massively consequential, and full of joy. Learning to live by the story of everything was, in short, learning a new life. "If anyone is in Christ," said Paul, unable even fully to finish his sentence before blurting out, "New Creation!" (2 Cor 5:17).

The next two chapters will explore the two main things that went with Christianity's surprise as it made its way into the world: the human and institutions.

Chapter 3
THE HUMAN

If any of the big questions is up for debate today, it is the question of what it is to be human.

When you think about it, it is a rather strange thing that we wonder what it is to be human. No other animal in all creation wonders what it is to be itself. A dog simply lives its life as a dog, doing whatever doggy things dogs do—and that's it. We live wondering who and what we are. The mere fact itself suggests that we do not instinctively know the answer. Were it apparent to us, we would not need to wonder. No search would be needed, no thought required. We would just know what it is to be human. But, instead, at whatever moment the human animal first experienced self-consciousness, we became mysteries to ourselves. And we have been reflecting on the human mystery—our self-mystery—ever since.

The story of everything tells us that our humanity is not something we can know simply by pursuing it, whether by philosophical reflection or scientific experiment or anything else. We can learn some important things, of course, but we cannot get the answer we seek, and we remain hidden from ourselves even in our self-pursuit. We are mysteries because we cannot help being so after the fall and until we are given the story that tells us who and what we are. Who and what we are, that is, must be revealed to us from beyond what we can ourselves come up with. In other words, humanity's self-understanding is a gift.

This "know who and what you are only by a gift" runs profoundly afoul of many strong contemporary narratives about human identity, in which we are told that we make our own stories about who we are. The story we believe is that we create our stories. We discover who we feel like we want to be, and we write our lives accordingly. "We" are the stories we write about ourselves—our desires, our relationships, our interests, our dreams, our victimization, our success . . . and on it goes. The story of everything, by contrast, tells us that our humanity is something given and has its origins and clarity not in what we take ourselves to be but in the way we were created and redeemed. Who and what we are, to put the point the other way around, requires telling the story of everything as our story. The question then becomes, When we do that, what emerges as the picture of the human?

The view of the human being that entered the world through Christian reflection on the significance of Jesus entailed a radical, new claim about what it is to be human. Indeed, so much so that we can speak of the Christian revelation of the human. Human beings had long been around, of course, but we were not yet what we became, and are called to become, in light of Christ. There were thus a great many things the early Christians had to learn in order to understand what we had become. From among these many things, four features of the overall picture stand out that are absolutely necessary to understand if we are to grasp the human as the Christians depicted it. We will take them in turn.

Jesus of Nazareth Is the Human

The most original and startling part of the early Christian view of the human is this: Jesus of Nazareth is the human. All other humans are his image.

In perhaps the most famous text from the book of Genesis, we read that the human was made in the "image of God," the Imago Dei (1:26-27). This passage was obviously read by Jews well before the time of Jesus, and they had long reflected on its significance. As a whole, Jewish interpretation of the Imago tended to say that the "image of God" was the

Jewish people. It was they who were in the world as God's image, as the reflection of the God of Israel and the way of life he desired.

Such an interpretation may appear somewhat strange to modern eyes since on the surface it looks like the Imago Dei text applies to all humans rather than just to the Jewish people. The Jewish reading is not strange, however, once one realizes that the interpretation depends on a reading of the scriptural narrative that moves chronologically from Adam to the election of Abraham and the formation of the Jewish people. Subsequent to Abraham, the scriptures told of Israel and not-Israel (the Gentiles or "Nations"). For the Jews who thought about it, the natural sense of the scriptural story is that human beings were made in God's image and then over time this image came to be focused upon and embodied within the people whom God subsequently chose to bear special witness to him. To put it differently, the Jewish interpretation took time and history seriously for the way the Imago was understood.

There is no special pleading here. Jewish readers were not searching for a timeless essence as the way to understand Adam but for a scripturally based developmental logic that made sense of their history as God's image-bearers. Modern interpreters of the Genesis stories tend to divide the text into bits and pieces of this or that tradition, and subsequently read the bits and pieces in isolation not only from one another but also from the rest of the biblical narrative. For ancient Jewish interpreters of Genesis, however, the scripture was not broken into diachronically unrelated parts but taken more as the unfolding of a complicated story. In short, according to the narrative logic of the Bible, Adam led to Israel. The Imago was, in a critical sense, uniquely and historically concentrated in the people who carried it forward in time.

Contrary to what one might initially imagine, the New Testament does not contradict this Jewish interpretation. Instead, it dramatically intensifies the notion that the Jewish elect bear God's image by focusing this image-bearing entirely on one Jew. Jewish history has indeed been the history of God's image, but this history has been moving toward its climax in a single point: Jesus is the elect one who is the witness to the God of Israel (1 Pet 2:4, 6; Luke 23:35, with dramatic irony). Indeed, there is no distance between them. The life of Jesus is God's life so much so that they share an identity as "Lord" (*Kyrios*). The Lord, that is, is none other than the Lord Jesus Christ. As the hymn in Philippians 2:5-11 puts it, Jesus now shares "the Name that is above all names," that is, *Kyrios*/Yahweh, so that "at the Name of Jesus every knee should bow, in heaven and on earth and under the earth, and every tongues confess that Jesus Christ is Lord [*Kyrios*], to the glory of God the Father" (vv. 10-11). At bottom, this shared identity is the reason that Jesus is said to be the image of God (2 Cor 4:4; Col 1:15). He is not God's image in the sense of a reflection that mirrors but does not capture the fullness of the real thing. He is instead the way God images himself in the history of creation and election. The total history of God's image, that is, has been aimed at this: God images himself fully and completely in Jesus of Nazareth. Jesus is the Imago Dei.

Thus is Jesus also the New Adam. As Luke and Paul thought, for example, to be God's image is to relive the creation depicted in Genesis 1:26-27 (Luke 3–4; Rom 5). In contradistinction to the Gospel of Matthew, for example, which traces Jesus's genealogy forward from Abraham through David to demonstrate Jesus's Jewish messianic credentials, the Gospel of Luke moves backward, from Jesus through David to Moses to Abraham to Seth to Adam, who was "the son of God." Luke's genealogy reaches back before the election of Israel and the division into Jew and Gentile to the original human, God's son, the one whom God made in his image. By means of this genealogical tracing, the story juxtaposes Jesus the Son of God and Adam the son of God. The point is not hard to discern: the Son of God has returned. Adam is figured in Jesus.

The theological purpose of the genealogy's placement in the narrative is also not difficult to discern for the simple fact that the immediately ensuing scene is the temptation. As the son of God once moved from advent to temptation, so the Son of God once again moves from advent to temptation. As the human son of God once carried the history of the human in his act, so the human Son of God once again carries the history of the human in his act. "*If* you are the Son of God . . ." the Devil begins, echoing loudly the question of obedience and decision that permeates the Genesis account (Luke 4:3). Jesus's subsequent resistance of the Devil, parrying of his moves, and resultant victory over him is, according to Luke's narrative, a new creation—the human redone, its possibilities renewed, its requirements amplified, and its true identity (re)disclosed. For the Gospel of Luke, as for Paul, the Adam—the human—is Jesus the Lord, the Son of God. As the story moves on and even into Acts, the Lord Jesus carries forward in his person what the human is, and thus reconfigures the understanding of humanity as that which exhibits the image of Adam-Christ.

The early Christian interpretation of the Genesis Imago text differed, therefore, from the typical non-Christian Jewish reading by going back to Adam to think through the implications of Jesus as the image of God. Biblical history did have a line of development, but this development moved not only from Adam to Israel but also from Israel to Adam. Which is to say that the early Christians worked with a complicated notion of time in which history was, as the church fathers would say with an all-important word, recapitulated.[1] They read forward but also backward: Adam the image led to Israel the image which led to Adam the image again. The Adam, that is, was the image of Jesus Christ all along, the one who had now come in time as Adam returned.

The exegesis of the Genesis Imago text had profound implications for what the Christians wanted to say about the human being itself. Since for the earliest Christians the image of God was not generic but specific and personal—Jesus Christ—the human beings that are in God's image are in God's image precisely because they are in the image of Jesus.

This is a "christological" interpretation of the human, which means that for the early Christians the most important thing that could be said about any and every human being was said with a name: Jesus Christ. In the New Testament and immediately beyond, there is no attempt to define the human apart from Jesus. It is not said, for example, that what makes a human being distinct from other earthly creatures is its rational faculty or unique physiology or moral grain (its capacity for right and wrong). All these things may well be said about human beings, but to make them a priori conditions of being human is to reason in abstraction from Jesus Christ. There is nothing strictly Christian about such general observations; they can be made—or disputed—by anyone at all. The earliest Christians, however, began with Jesus and said that whenever you encounter a human being you simultaneously encounter him. Such particularizing had never before appeared in history.

In the context of a modernity that has taught us to think of the human in terms of essences or rational capacities or desires—or many other things besides—the New Testament speaks a different and surprising word: to think the question of the human is to think Jesus Christ. The Imago Dei language in Genesis 1 is taken to mean that, at bottom, the image in whose image the human is made is that of the Son of God, Jesus. How interesting, then, that we have flesh. The human shows up enfleshed because, after all, the Son of God is in time the human Jesus. To be made in his image is to have flesh. When we see the human enfleshed, we see the image of Christ. With that thought, we turn to the other side of the question.

Humans Are "Christ"

The logic was uncomplicated but profound and its implications staggering: because Jesus Christ is the human, every human is Jesus Christ. Historically considered, this was nothing less than a *novum* in the conception of humanity as such.

The classifications of the human in the Roman world were enormously varied and complicated, as were the different philosophical options on offer. Not one of them, however, read the human figurally in light of a central guiding person to whom all people were related, and not one of them, therefore, took all humans to be exactly what they were in relation to that figure. Moreover, none of the philosophical options interpreted the human being so that it meant the same thing in every instance. There were always the "barbarians" of one sort or another. Even Stoicism, for all its supposed emphasis on the equality of the human as a potential philosophical apprentice, assumed some radical differences when thinking through the actual discrepancies in human life.

The reach of the Christian view of the human was humanity. There were no exceptions. Humanity is one—one in Adam, one in the New Adam. Because the human is conceived as the image of Jesus Christ, there is no place where humans are—or are *from*—that lies outside of Christ and where the "human being" would thus be something less or other than fully human. Inasmuch as he relates to all creation as the one through whom all creation came to be, all humans who exist are in his image. Baptism effects outwardly and publicly what is true of the human in Christ. As Paul famously—and startlingly—put it to the baptized Christians in the churches of Galatia: "there is neither Jew nor Gentile, slave nor free, male and female; for you all are one in Christ Jesus" (Gal 3:28). Though many today read this verse as underwriting specific causes of various kinds, its real thrust is much deeper: in the face of all divisions of humanity past and present into greater and lesser or more and less human, Galatians echoes Genesis 1 to say once again that there really is no *human* difference in Christ.

Jesus himself began the work of this envisioning. He knew that our inability to see the human on the other side of our inherited and well-maintained lines of division was severe and could not simply be lectured away. He therefore engaged in transformational and embodied story-telling, or, to put it slightly differently, a variety of "work-arounds": from parables to perfectly staged, provoking healings to extremely awkward dinner parties to prophetic rebuke. All were intended to disassemble the received categories of "human" and reconfigure them in light of God's inbreaking kingdom. The most famous work-around is probably the parable of the good Samaritan.

The parable occurs only in Luke's Gospel and encapsulates many uniquely Lukan themes (Luke 10:25-37). A long-popular reading of the parable takes the summary injunction—"go and do likewise"—to apply generally in this way: go be a good person like the Samaritan (and negatively, do not be like the passersby). To be sure, every culture can always use more such people, but the point of the parable is actually something else. The key lies in the questions posed by the lawyer that elicits the parable and by Jesus at the end that requires the lawyer to answer his own question.

The lawyer's question, "who is my neighbor?" (v. 29), is not the feeble comeback it is often taken to be. For first-century Jews, doing what the law required meant being clear about how to fulfill its commandments in practice. If the law says that one is to love your neighbor, one needs to know who counts as "neighbor." Defining "neighbor" means that one then knows what to do because one knows exactly whom to love. "OK, so we are to love our neighbor. But who's the neighbor?" The lawyer asks Jesus to be specific.

As with many of his parables, Jesus constructs the scene to lead the hearer's expectations in a direction that he subsequently subverts or complicates. In this case, the parable unfolds with the expectation that the "neighbor" is the one who has been violently robbed, the priest and the Levite those who do not love their neighbor as they should, and the Samaritan the one who exemplifies the love of neighbor. Given the extremely poor relations between Jews and Samaritans in the first century, this in itself would be surprising to Jewish sensibilities,[2] but Jesus's precisely phrased question turns things in a different direction: "which of these three seems to you to have become a neighbor to the man who fell among the bandits?" (10:36). By asking the lawyer who the victim's neighbor was, Jesus does not require the lawyer to draw the conclusion that the victim is his neighbor—that he may well already assume—but that the *Samaritan* is his neighbor. The lawyer, however, cannot quite bring himself to say "Samaritan," though he obviously knows the answer. He says instead, "the one who showed him mercy." This answer dismantles and rebuilds the categories the lawyer employs when thinking of the meaning of neighbor and works on the level of affect to draw the circle of neighbor as wide as it can get. By the end of the parable the lawyer now has to include the repugnant Samaritan when he gives the answer to his own question, Who is my neighbor? The force of the parable, therefore, is not a simple "be good like the unlikely character the Samaritan" but "Samaritans are your neighbors. Show them mercy." This, one might say, is a parabolic rendition of Adam/Christ theology. No one is "not-neighbor."

The anthropological assumption that grounds "the Samaritan is your neighbor" teaching depends on the sense that "Samaritan" is now included within what is meant by the image of Jesus. The Samaritans, too, fit in the genealogy of the S/son of God.

Such a vision of the human entailed a posture, an ethic, a way of being in the world with other humans whom you knew to be Christ. Again, it was Jesus himself who initiated the church's human ethic.

In the last of Jesus's major teaching sections in the Gospel of Matthew, he tells several parables, concluding them—and his teaching as a whole—with a whopper: the sheep and the goats. The imagery used here to speak of the future judgment is intended to shock and unsettle, and the parable's point for the present is to engender action. It is straightforward and clear: care for the poor with your actions and you're a sheep; care not for the poor with your actions and you're a goat. The first way is blessing and life; the second, judgment and death. What is most striking for our purposes, however, is the anthropological claim embedded in the parable, that which gives the parable its sense and force as a command for Christian action and discipleship.

When in the parable the king says, "I was hungry and you gave me food, I was thirsty and you gave me drink, I was a stranger and you welcomed me, I was naked and you clothed me, I was sick and you visited me, I was in prison and you came to me," he begins a radical identification between king and the lowly (Matt 25:35-36). The question then comes, "But when did we see you a stranger and welcome you, or naked and clothe you? And when did we see you sick or in prison and visit you?" Though perhaps too familiar to us, when read afresh, the king's answer is absolutely astonishing, "Truly, I say to you, as you did it to one of the least of these my brothers, you did it to me" (Matt 25:40). Citizens of modern liberal democracies typically must struggle immensely to imagine what a true king was in all his power and splendor, but in the ancient world everyone knew that to say the king was lowly was to say water was dry, a snail was fast, an attacking lion harmless, Nero nice, Domitian docile. The contradiction was as blatant as contradictions come. The parable turns, in fact, on this drastic contradiction and the picture of the human it presupposes and engenders.

The parable requires a much more specific anthropological understanding than a simple "representation," namely, the poor, destitute, and imprisoned represent something more than their mere appearance would initially suggest. The king speaks of a closeness of kinship that means the lowly are so much the king's family that when they are encountered, the king himself is encountered. In short, they bear his image. When one encounters the lowly, therefore, one sees the image of the king, and they are to be treated as one would treat the king. The lowly, as it turns out, are nothing less than kingly. Which is to say that the lowly are the image of Jesus, who is obviously the king.

In time, the interpretation of the parable made the connections between Jesus/the king/the beggars explicit: the human—from kings to beggars—is in the form of Christ. Peter was what the Roman centurion Cornelius was. The slave Onesimus was what the master Philemon was. Philemon was what the Roman governor Sergius Paulus was. The low and the high were bound together in their humanity precisely because their humanity was and is constituted in Christ.

No one reading early Christian literature could think that this monumental shift in the understanding of human beings brought an instant end to all forms of prejudice or classifications that ran crosswise to the Christian vision. The first really sizable fight in the church that we know about, in fact, occurred across ethnic/cultural lines. The Aramaic-speaking Christians ("the Hebrews") neglected the needs of the widows among the Greek-speaking Christians ("the Hellenists"). The church leaders found a solution to the practical problem, of course, but the deeper point at stake was how to envision the widow across the ethnic/cultural line from you as the human you knew her to be in Christ. Samaritans no less than Galileans or Judeans. Greeks no less than Jews. Hutus no less than Tutsis. Blacks no less than whites.

In the next chapter on "institutions" we will see some of the more significant ways in which this ethic/posture was lived by the church and its social extensions. For now, however, the point is the anthropology that underlies all ecclesial action called love of neighbor is christological through and through. Humanity is reconceived as one in light of who Jesus is and that he has now come. In terms of the story of everything, the effect of Jesus's resurrection is new creation on display, at work in the world.

Human Sin and Transformation

It would be all too easy to understand this new view of the human as a fantasy or, perhaps, an optimist's version of extreme optimism. This is what we dream or desire or confidently project ourselves to be even though we really know we're not. For the early Christians, nothing could be farther from the truth. They knew from the story of everything that the human that is Christ's image exists in a world that is not yet fully redeemed and that we actively participate in this "not yet." The "not yet" was—and is—in plain sight. Our attempts to see others as Christ is a true north, a vision for what humanity truly is, but our action will always be in danger of betraying this vision. In short, we continue to sin and to experience the deforming effects of sin's power. We therefore need repentance, forgiveness, and transformation as vital parts of what it is to be human. The human is a thing that needs to repent, to be forgiven, and to be transformed.

If Paul speaks of the human as the image of Adam/Christ, he also obviously understands the power of the Adam that we have been. The entirety of the Corinthian correspondence, for example, is painful testimony to residual patterns of the old Adam in the life of the early Christians. They fight, they divide, they act immorally, they return to pagan festivals, they mistreat the poor at the Lord's Supper, they accuse Paul of weakness, they glory in themselves, and much more besides. And if Luke believes that the terms of being human have been reset by the obedience of the Son of God in the desert, he also narrates the history of the church as one of sin and complicated struggle to become that which we have been freed to be. No reader of the scheming of Ananias and Sapphira, or the massive disagreement in Jerusalem over the place of the Gentiles in the church, or the heated argument and split between Paul and Barnabas, and so on, could imagine an immediate or perfect synonymy between the Son of God and the Adam who initially went astray.

Indeed, every time the famous parable of the tax collector and the Pharisee was read in the church, the remainder of the old Adam was on display and held forth as honest commentary on the human: stand at a distance from the holy and cry out, "God, be merciful to me a sinner!" (Luke 18:13). Every time Jesus's words about the practice of forgiveness were read and repeated, the old Adam's indelible print was clearly seen on fellow travelers ("a brother"): "If your brother sins against you, and if he repents, forgive him. Even if he sins against you seven times a day and seven times returns to you and says, 'I repent,' you will forgive him" (Luke 17:3-4). Matthew makes it even clearer: "'Lord,'" says Peter, "'how often shall I forgive my brother when he sins against me? As many as seven times?' And Jesus said to him: 'I do not say to you "as many as seven times" but as many as seventy times seven'" (Matt 18:21-22). Adam and Adam and Adam again. Indeed, contrary to both ancient and modern Christian heresies that believe in one way or another that the new age has completely overtaken the old, the New Testament always shows a human who is "Adam-and-not-Adam" at once. Never is it even hinted that we are only the new Adam and cannot show the old. To the contrary, the New Testament speaks of the power of transformation and the practices that go with a people being transformed: repentance and forgiveness. Without frank acknowledgment of the sin, we are dreamers. Without forgiveness for that sin, we are lost and trapped in the guilt and shame that only forgiveness can free us from. We are Adam and on the way to Adam. We are new creation and stumble still. We blow it and blow it again and yet are being transformed into the new image we were always meant to be.

Paul puts the point precisely in his exhortation to the Colossians not to lie to one another. The reason to be truthful is that they have "taken off the old *Adam* with his practices and put on the new one, the one who is being renewed in knowledge according to the Image of his creator" (Col 3:9-10). Even the Corinthians, who obviously have a long, long way to go, have actually come a long way to become a living testimony to transformation into the Lord's image (2 Cor 3:18). And the church in Rome is counseled not to exist in conformation with the old patterns ("this age") but to be "transformed by the renewal of the mind" (Rom 12:2). The transformation will not happen all at once; it is a process and one whose fruit is "to exhibit genuine love, to hate what is evil, to hold onto what is good . . . to be aglow in the Spirit and to serve the Lord . . . to contribute to the needs of the saints and practice hospitality" (Rom 12:9-13).

If, as Charles Taylor has persuasively argued, the absence of the belief in the possibility of human transformation—a fundamental remaking of a human life-trajectory in light of transcendent goods—is one of the defining marks of our current age, then our age's prevailing view is exactly opposite of the early Christians. They knew of and endorsed many earthly goods (marriage, children, friendship, etc.), of course, but their view of the human is transformational through and through. In order to deal with the reality of ongoing sin in the human image of God, and thus to be and become ourselves—the human as we were made and redeemed to be—we must undergo transformation into that image. For the human to emerge as the Imago of God is for it to be remade in the image of Christ.[3]

Death and Life: What Is Our Future?

Understanding Jesus Christ as the human and the human as Jesus Christ results in a variety of life-giving practices. But the truth is that if death is the final word on human life, these practices would all be pointless in the face of its power. If death ultimately wins, the story of everything is a story of nothing, and the view of the human that entered the world with Jesus and the early Christians is romantic nonsense. We would simply be telling ourselves sentimental stories about why we don't need to be afraid, and meaninglessly moralizing in the face of our insignificance, extinction, and nothingness. We long to live, but that longing would eventually be extinguished, even mocked, shown by empirical fact to be a flaw in the one and only species on the planet that knows what is in store for it. Death is exactly that which comments on our humanity with unfailing and indisputable accuracy. We will all die. Whether that is the final and most powerful word about us or not is the question.

The earliest Christians were crystal clear about this. They had none of our current inhibitions that lead us to find ever-stranger ways to talk around death or avoid talking about it at all. Indeed, at the center of the New Testament stands a death, that of Jesus of Nazareth. The four Gospels themselves are, as Martin Kähler once quipped, essentially passion narratives with long introductions.[4] No more than the messiah avoided his crucifixion, thought the original Christians, can we avoid our encounter with decay and death. His story ran from birth toward death, and thus so does ours. We are Adam, as Paul puts it, and "all die" (1 Cor 15:22).

But precisely because the story of everything teaches Christians to think "human" in light of Christ, precisely because his story is our story, we learn to think of our deaths as a penultimate word—real, painful, grief-filled, but penultimate nevertheless. Jesus's pattern is ours: life, death, then resurrection. Which is to say that his future is our future and that our link to him through our humanity is our hope. In him, we see our future beyond death. Hope is thus the mark of an existence that faces the truth of death but hangs everything on the resurrection. We really do grieve at death, says Paul, but not as those who have no hope (1 Thess 4:13). Or as the little letter 1 Peter straightforwardly puts it, "we have been born anew to a living hope through the resurrection of Jesus Christ from the dead" (1 Pet 1:3).

By thinking through the significance of our humanity in light of Jesus's resurrection, the early Christians came to see that on the other side of certain human death lies a victory, life; the first Adam may well hang on every human till the end, but the Last Adam has made it true that "also in Christ shall all be made alive" (1 Cor 15:22). As Paul says to the Romans about the significance of their baptism for their future, "For if we have been united with him in a death like his, we shall certainly be united with him in a resurrection like his" (Rom 6:5).

Indeed, the entire point of the Gospel of John—if we may be bold enough to summarize it—is to trust in the eternal life given by Jesus Christ in the face of death. "Lord," Peter asks, voicing for the reader the reason to read the Gospel at all, "to whom shall we go? You have the words of eternal life" (John 6:68; cf. 3:15-16; 3:36; 4:14, 36). The letter 1 John makes it

48

even plainer: Jesus Christ is "eternal life" (1 John 5:20). Those who trust in him receive the "promise," which is "eternal life" (1 John 2:25).

All of early Christianity pulsates with the hope of eternal life. This hope was what funded the willingness to be persecuted and martyred, to nurse the sick and dying even if it meant catching deadly diseases, to start hospitals, to sacrifice possessions, to speak boldly to Roman authorities, and countless other matters. Modern psychologists have wondered about people like Paul or Ignatius of Antioch or Polycarp or other early martyrs and tried to understand them in terms of theories about altruism or social cost/benefit behavior, and so forth. But all of that simply ignores the reason the texts plainly give for such behavior in favor of something more suitable to a modern palate (a palate whose taste is only for that within the immanent frame). The texts show that the early Christians saw death as a rock-bottom reality of human life—the end of temporal life that we can plainly if painfully see—and trusted that they would be raised to eternal life on the other side of their deaths. Their action is not mysterious, even if it is out of keeping with what average human beings normally do. It is fully and clearly intelligible: they acted exactly in line with the hope of the resurrection.

The New Testament texts claim that this hope is now actively written into the human Imago by virtue of the last Adam's life-creating resurrection (1 Cor 15:45). To be God's image—as Adam and Adam remade—is thus to have a future in God's own future. This is the extension of the claim for human transformation, its perfection and end: "we shall all be transformed . . . [and] when the perishable puts on the imperishable, and the mortal puts on the immortal, then what is written shall happen: Death is swallowed up in Victory" (1 Cor 15:54).

Insofar, therefore, as we learn how to be Christian, we learn our future in the midst of the present. The "image's imaging of the Image" is ultimately a witness to the power of God's life in a world of death, a witness to the victory that will come in the middle of a present that will temporarily defeat us, a witness to grace in the midst of sin, and a witness to a final gift of life in a world that always takes it away.

Conclusion

The Christian vision of the human was radical. It was new. And it erupted into Mediterranean culture in surprising ways.

Aside from the intimations of the human in ancient Judaism, the Roman world had no understanding of the human being that is even analogous to the Christian vision. When one enters the realm of metaphysical reflection—what is a soul, what is a body, how do they relate to each other if in fact they are different, and so on—there were of course all kinds of interesting connections to philosophical thought of a variety of types. But in terms of the actual thing that shows up in the world, the thing that we are and have to deal with in different but similar instantiations—other people!—there was nothing even close to the human as the Christians understood it. The phenomenon *human*—how we appear as a distinct thing to ourselves, and how others appear to us as humans, what the "human" is that shows up in the actual living of life—this is the new, radical thing that emerged with Christianity. The earliest Christians claimed that Jesus Christ revealed what the human was and where it was headed. And from there the vision of the human that emerged with the earliest Christians has never disappeared.

In the next chapter on "institutions" we will see how the early Christians put the human into the world in concrete ways; for them, the thing that was the human required social and political explication as a witness to God's work in Christ and as a way to keep the vision of the human alive through time. If the vision of the human were not lived in real time, as it were, that which it had become could not survive, develop staying power, and grow.

For now, however, the major point to make is that though we don't typically recognize it, the vision of the human as the image of God's image is the vision that has marked all subsequent ethics in the West down through the ages. It is implicit in the daily work we do in places like hospitals, orphanages, and various charities, and it lies behind what seems self-evident and what we take for granted in a wide swath of contemporary life.

For example, in wider society we systematically care for the sick who are not our own—under the assumption that the human requires care even when we are unrelated by blood or marriage. We argue ferociously over how best to safeguard one another and even utter strangers from one sort of harm or another—under the assumption that the human is the sort of thing that demands our moral reasoning and protection regardless of tribe allegiance or loyalties. We have compassion on and look out for children who have been orphaned—under the assumption that the "orphan" is a particular sort of human that demands care. We say that you cannot force people to believe against their conscience what they simply can't or won't believe—under the assumption that the human has a conscience that is God-given and/or inviolable. We condemn genocide, racism, and other evil acts based on tribe, physiognomy, or history—under the assumption that the human is unified at a basic level and is not the kind of thing that can be divided and grouped in these ways for destruction. We think the poor or the homeless are people who require response, help, mercy—under the assumption that the human can be seen in them as in us and that they can legitimately hope for help from other members of their common family. We are scandalized by lies in the public square—under the assumption that the human being is bound to truth and is not the sort of thing that can be purposefully deceived, lied to without harm.

We assume such things, and many more like them, not because their truth is actually self-evident or simply out there for anyone to look at and see. Indeed, the history of human behavior is one giant and long-running negation of the idea that human dignity and its corresponding practices are self-evident (or, if ever seen, easy to practice). The Imago may glint and glimmer here and there, but as a whole we have displayed a stunning recklessness and cruelty with human life of all kinds and on all scales. Our current moral hopes and practices make sense, therefore, because we presuppose a conception of the human being funded by centuries of Christian thought and practice. We take their truth for granted, that is, because we take for granted much of what the human is and how it is thus to be treated. Change the conception of the human being, and the obligations and norms that go with it change, too.

We also lament the hypocrisy of the church, crying out in the face of its sins against the people it is meant to shelter and heal. The hypocrisy itself, however, is only identifiable as hypocrisy because we already have a background set of assumptions about what the church considers the human truly to be and how it is to act toward that human, and we interpret the church's behavior against that background of assumptions. Absent this background, hypocrisy is not hypocrisy at all but merely the way the church behaves. The hypocrisy is all the more severe because the standards by which the church, and Christians, should be measured are so crucial. The treachery against human beings is specifically hypocritical because of what the human is in Christ.

In a way that has not been true since its entrance into the world, the human in the Christian sense is currently imperiled. During its long history it has often been under direct attack philosophically and through practices that obviously throw mud in its face, such as infanticide, but what is more recent—and, in an important sense, more alarming and more seductive—is what we might paradoxically call the moral attack. The moral attack is the current way almost an entire culture believes it can sustain basic moral commitments that derive from the Christian view of the human without the Christianity that introduced those commitments to begin with because of what it took the human to be. The moral attack basically assumes that we've learned what we needed to learn about ethics, and can now discard the religious husk in which the moral kernel was historically contained. Keep the morality, chuck the Christianity.

This is seductive precisely because it attempts to hold on to what it would frighten us to let go of and because it makes us appear to ourselves as good and kind. We look into the mirror, feel virtuous, and can smile. The magnitude of what is at stake is hidden behind our self-assurances that we are good people and will produce a culture of moral commitments as rich as or richer than the ones we have inherited from the Christians. We justify the cavalier attitude toward Christianity by telling ourselves that the goods the Christians have historically delivered will not go away even if their religious origins do.

What most people don't know is that this has already been tried. In the fourth century the Roman emperor Julian renounced and subsequently detested the Christian faith, but he retained an admiration for the works of charity that Christian communities promoted and exhibited. In a well-known letter to one of his pagan high priests, Julian mentioned his distrust of the motivation of the "Galileans" but noted that they were kind "to strangers" and "support not only their poor but ours as well; everyone can see that our people lack aid from us."[5] Julian the Apostate, as later tradition would call him, therefore harassed Christians while at the same time setting about trying to energize Roman pagans to produce their own philanthropic works. It failed. Absent the sense that the human is the image of Christ and that by attending to the human we attend to Christ, absent the sense that the human requires our care regardless of the difference between friend and stranger, absent the sense that the human can be seen for what it is only through extensive social and political display—absent all this and more—there is nothing to keep the specifically Christian works alive. Julian's pagan revival had no ground to stand on. He could not make people care simply by declaring that they should, nor could he jump-start good works by attempting to ignite pagan religious life. The whole project was a flop: retaining Christian life and a vision of what it means to be human without the Christianity was impossible.

What Julian discovered in antiquity is the point that Nietzsche and Sartre made sharp in the modern world: as a whole, all that's needed to defeat moralizing is simply to ignore it and go your own way. You do not have to provide a single reason, a single argument, a single justification. You just do what you want. The moralizers may cry foul, may indignantly cough and splutter, may accuse you of all kinds of nasty-sounding things, and may demand an answer with all the emotion they can muster. But you do not have to give them one. You can simply ignore them, or laugh at them, or mock them if you like, or flip them the bird, or do whatever pleases you. There is nothing to bind you, nothing to call you, nothing to oblige you. Morality by itself is a fiction and utterly uncompelling. If there's no God, no resurrection of Jesus Christ, and therefore no human in the Christian sense, then there is no reason to treat other people as

53

Christianity has argued you should. The moralizers are fooling themselves and, truth be told, simply too cowardly to face a world without their morals, a world in which the human is only what it makes of and for itself—which is, of course, a world in which the cleverest and strongest among us always win. Nihilism, that is, will easily win, every time.

The lesson that we could learn from Julian is the critical one that we cannot sustain the moral commitments that lie behind many of our most basic practices that we pour time and money into and laud as examples of human excellence without the Christianity that makes such morality make sense in the first place. Theology and ethics are in the end really just one thing. It may take a while, of course, even a long while, but eventually without the Christian vision of the human, the ethics that go with it will disappear, too. (We already see it vanishing to a startling degree, for example, in those who support infanticide but use the Orwellian language "late-term abortion.") In order to retain the human as it has come to be in time, therefore, we will have to retain that which brought this human into the world in the first place.

"Retaining" the human, however, is hardly a matter of the mind alone, as if we could simply remember, articulate, and disseminate the idea. It has to have traction in the world, take up social space, and make itself known and felt in behaviors that embody, interpret, and project the Christian understanding of the human for the world to see. At the beginning, the story that required Christians to understand Jesus as the human and the human as Christ simultaneously required them to develop means of making these truths come true in practice—which made the truth of the human appear in the Roman world as palpable witness. In short, as the earliest Christians knew well, maintaining and manifesting the human necessitates institutions. The institutions were what took the Christian vision of the human public.

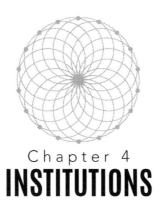

Chapter 4

INSTITUTIONS

Today we almost automatically think of institutions as bureaucratic extinguishers of vibrant faith and all that goes into them—dynamic relationships, powerful worship, works of justice, and imaginative thinking. If you want to slow, or stop, the beating heart of new faith, institutionalize it. If you want to oppress human beings, build institutions that smother their natural creativity. If you want to ensure that innovation never gets the upper hand, do things in an institution. If you want drudgery day after day, work in an institution. And so on.

The early Christians did not share our view. Instead, they insisted that the revelation of the human required the development of institutions to sustain the practices that kept the new vision of the human visible and alive in the world. The story of everything positioned them, that is, as institutionally creative people. For them, the question was not whether to build or get rid of institutions, but what kind of institutions Christianity requires to spread the surprising good news and to live it out through time.

The immediate answer the earliest Christians gave to the question of how best to carry forward the mission of Jesus was the church. This answer is as likely to startle us as it did the French biblical scholar Alfred Loisy, who famously once wrote, "Christ announced the Kingdom and it is the church that came."[1] However he originally intended it in 1902, Loisy's statement now reads like a summary of much contemporary sentiment about institutions when applied to the church: the church is at best a poor substitute for the kingdom of God, a real step down from the charisma and vision of Jesus. Originally, so it is frequently thought, church was not an institution but a more intimate, less hierarchical, free-flowing style of community.

The truth, however, is mostly otherwise. There was real charisma at the beginning, but the origins of the church as institution actually lie with Jesus himself. Jesus chose twelve apostles to symbolize the ingathering of the twelve tribes of Israel, the reconstitution of God's people in the congregation who testified to his new work in history. After Jesus's resurrection, his followers saw the urgency of the symbol, and elected Matthias to fill Judas Iscariot's place. The fact that we never hear of Matthias again makes clear the importance attached to the wholeness of the body of Jesus's followers from the very earliest days. It was more important to symbolize and maintain the trajectory of the community through its leadership structure than it was to relate individual biographies.

Many current movements that wish to get away from "institutionalized" Christianity look to the book of Acts for their inspiration. Their sense is that the Holy Spirit is poured out at Pentecost, and the church follows the Spirit's prompting from then on and flourishes. Since the church was alive in the Spirit, there was no need for an institution. The community was led, it cohered, and it grew. Institutionalized religion is nowhere in sight, and had it come about, it would have stifled the Spirit's work.

While it is true that the Spirit guides the Christians in Acts and that Pentecost marks a surprise eruption of the Spirit into the world, the anti-institutional interpretation is a misreading of the story and of early Christianity as a whole. Indeed, it is historically indefensible. As Acts tells it, not only did the earliest Christians begin their movement with ecclesial structure (the twelve), they learned immediately that a lack of order did not mean freedom; it meant disorder. Early on, a prominent couple tried to deceive the community about their possessions, for example, and Greek-speaking widows were neglected in favor of those who spoke Aramaic, the "first" language of Judea (Acts 5–6).

Deceiving the community about possessions and neglecting a group of widows were major threats to the early Christian community precisely because they threatened the vision of the human that came with Jesus. Christians could not image the Image while simultaneously refusing to be generous and neglecting widows in need. In terms of the story of everything, the church learned that even after the resurrection the fall was still with us, and even though we could learn to be generous we would also be tricky, selfish, and chauvinistic. Carrying forward the surprising news was a fragile business and demanded hard thought and creative practice to keep it alive for the world to see.

Before moving on, we need to make a crucial point about the word *institution* and what it's meant to convey in this chapter. The early Christians were not primarily thinking "about institutions," as if what interested them were institutions *per se* or organizational structures or legacies. They were not the forerunners of modern social scientists who analyze institutions already in existence or consultants or coaches who seek to improve what is already there. Instead, the earliest Christians were "thinking institutionally," which means that they were thinking through the basic issues of their common life and mission with a series of important questions: What things do we have to have in place to be and remain who we are and why we exist? What must be retained from what we already have, and what must be newly developed? What habits do we have to cultivate in our people and how do we get these habits into practice in an environment of rapid growth? In short, what *must* be there for us to be us?[2]

The earliest Christians answered these questions with an astonishing array of activities, habits, and innovations. Three broad areas stand out, however, as particularly important when trying to get a picture of Christianity's initial surprise in the world: structure, education, and care. The three areas were not isolated from one another in the life of the early church; in fact, they were inseparably intertwined and all related to what it meant for the church to be and remain the church. Treating them separately, however, allows some of their distinctive features to emerge more clearly.

57

Structure and Hierarchy

To state the obvious: the church did not drop from heaven fully formed with bishops, elders, deacons, and so on. Yet order was remarkably quick in coming. Jesus's selection of the Twelve set a leadership trajectory that was followed into the post-resurrection period. Not only had they been with Jesus in his earthly ministry, the disciples were also instructed by him after his resurrection for "forty days"—the time echoing Moses's reception of the Torah and, hence, signaling the inauguration of the New Covenant. The Twelve were thus the ones whose "authoritative teaching" (*didachē*) was what the church learned for the simple but crucial reason that they had authority in matters of history and content (esp. Acts 2 and 4). Among them, Peter and John stood out as leaders among leaders, and, though not one of the Twelve, the "Lord's brother" James became a principal authority in Jerusalem (according to Paul, the resurrected Jesus had appeared personally to James, presumably for just such a purpose; 1 Cor 15:7).

After his encounter with Jesus, the Apostle Paul initially struck out on his own. But, after a time, even he went to Jerusalem to make sure he had not "run in vain" (Gal 2:2). Paul did not doubt that he knew the truth of the gospel (Gal 1), but he also knew that such truth would stand in continuity with the Lord's chosen disciples or not stand at all.

Almost immediately the church grew large enough to begin providing for its vulnerable members. The widows were chief among them. But some of the early Christians initially saw widows in two classes. There were the widows who were culturally more Palestinian ("Aramaic-speaking") and the widows who were less so ("Greek-speaking"). The former ranked above the latter, some apparently thought, and the latter could thus be neglected if push came to shove (giving the neglectors a better motive rather than worse). Over time this neglect became a crisis, one that threatened the unity of the church and was replete with infighting, gossip, and all the rest (Luke's use of *gongusmos*—murmuring, complaining—in Acts 6:1 is a discretionary understatement; he says it this way on purpose, but we can read between the lines easily enough).

58

One of the strong indicators of a well-functioning structure is when the leaders are able to solve complex problems creatively in a crisis without becoming fully enmeshed in the workings of the solution itself. Such was the case with the widow crisis. The Twelve summoned the main players in the conflict, sized up the problem, and realized that additional leadership structure was needed to solve it. The apostolic office required the Twelve to continue doing what they were already doing, and it was not enough simply to lecture the groups into new practice; new structure was needed. Thus was born the office of deacon. The selection of seven men who were known for their witness, their Spirit-filled life, and their wisdom was the way the church tied purpose to structure and said—implicitly of course but publicly, too—that structure was not simply a practical solution. It was also a way of holding forth for the world to see the kind of institution that the church was becoming.

The office of deacon was widespread but it took longer to develop than that of bishop (*episcopos*) and elder (*presbyteros*). The elders were leaders in Jerusalem from the earliest days and already by the time of Paul's final journey had been established in major Christian communities such as Ephesus. The elders from the Ephesian church, for example, come out to Miletus to meet Paul on his way to Jerusalem for the last time (Acts 20). The New Testament traditions about the roles of elders and bishops show the office in flux as they initially came to be, but by the time of Ignatius of Antioch in the early second century the elder and bishop had become distinct offices. Ignatius himself was a bishop and stood at the head of the elders. Among other letters that show his relation to his churches, he wrote a letter to Polycarp, the bishop of Smyrna in Asia Minor, who kissed Ignatius's chains as Ignatius was led to Rome as a prisoner. Both bishops were eventually martyred. From Ignatius on, the offices of bishops and the elders were permanent features of the developing church.

In the Age of Democracy, it can be hard to remember how important a bishop was. We tend to think that everything important requires a vote and that the mere presence of an authority figure somehow interferes with the flourishing of a community. For the earliest Christians, things were otherwise. The bishop was critical to the community's identity through time and for its unity across the Mediterranean. The bishop was the pastor, spiritual guide, doctrinal educator, and glue between various churches. So much so that, as Robert Wilken once observed, there is no evidence of any "enduring Christian communit[y]" without a tie to a bishop.[3]

Over time, the bishops argued and fought with one another; strong leaders often do. But the important point to realize is that without the development of the structure that means "institution" in a significant sense, the ability to sustain a common life and mission would not have existed. The leadership structure ensured that even when arguments were intense, the disputants could count on the fact that they were disputing within and about a shared framework of life. (Heresy was not so much disagreement on this or that point of doctrine as it was a break with the framework.) Not until a millennium into its existence when East and West could not reconcile did the institutional structure face a fundamentally serious challenge—and then half a millennium later when Martin Luther's reforms led to establishments far beyond what he originally intended. But even in each of these times of monumental upheaval in the church, the resultant division involved at least a quasi-replication of the original structure. There were, to be sure, massive adjustments in how bishops, elders, and deacons were understood in the different Protestant groups that emerged, but even those most suspicious of the structure of institutions, the "govern by consensus" Quakers, discovered the need for "clerks" to guide their meetings and "executive committees" to direct them at national levels.

It would be a mistake, however, were we to think of ecclesial structure in crudely pragmatic terms, as if the only real work structure does is to answer practically the question of how to organize new communities. Developing particular offices within the church was, of course, important for organization. Indeed, though this is seldom said aloud today, community always requires hierarchy of one sort or another. But the work structure did for the earliest Christians went far beyond mere pragmatic solutions and enabled the Christians to cultivate a political identity as *Christians* in distinction from the state. No governing official had any say in who became bishop; nor were the bishops officials of their cities. Their authority was determined only by the Christian community itself. Rather than just being another funeral or fireman's club or a philosophical school—things the Romans initially thought about organized groups of Christians—the early church became a distinct sort of society with its own norms and chains of authority. In short, the structure enabled the church to lay its own political ground, and that ground, in turn, enabled the perception of the critical difference between church and world. And *that* in its turn enabled the Christians to see the question of ultimate loyalty that was at stake in the demand not to worship the emperor or other gods, come what may. To which community did you *really* belong? The institution, not simply the idea, of church built the terms of the choice. As one of the church's initial critics, Celsus, saw clearly, the early Christians had refused the terms that took it for granted that all religion was tied to Roman authority. They were building their own thing.

And to do that, they needed to know and to remember who they were. In other words, they needed to be educated.

Education

The earliest recorded descriptions of what it meant to be the church tell us that the Christians devoted themselves to the *didachē*—the teaching, the instruction—of the apostles (Acts 2 and 4). One was not born into the world with the knowledge necessary to be Christian. Being Christian was something that had to be learned. And this meant, of course, that someone had to teach it.

Jesus himself was often called "teacher" (*didaskalos* = rabbi). He taught from start to finish and even after his resurrection. The early Christians learned from him that they, too, had to teach. When Luke writes the preface to his Gospel, for example, he tells Theophilus that the narrative he will read will confirm the truth of the things in which he has been catechized (*katēcheō*). The church in Antioch, where the early Christians were first actually called "Christians," had teachers (Acts 13:1). Paul speaks of "teachers" alongside other roles (apostles and prophets, for example), and the pastoral letters in the Pauline tradition show an intense concern for

61

the right teachers who teach the right things, namely "faith and truth," as 1 Timothy 2:7 puts it.

By the close of the first century, teaching became so important that several New Testament texts warn of the danger of false teaching that could lead the Christian communities astray, and they emphasize the corresponding necessity of "sound teaching" (2 Tim, Titus, 2 Pet). The little but highly potent letter of James recognizes the gravity of teaching Christian truth and warns its readers about becoming teachers. "Let not many of you become teachers, brothers, knowing that we shall receive a greater judgment" (Jas 3:1). Precisely because of what they claimed was at stake in teaching faith and truth, the early Christians knew that teachers bear more responsibility than those who are taught.

As best as we can tell from the sources that come immediately after the New Testament texts—the *Didache*, the *Shepherd of Hermas*, the *Epistle of Barnabas*, and so on—most of the teaching took place in ecclesial settings rather than in official Christian schools that stood alone and existed simply for the purpose of education. Worship, preparation for baptism, and common assembly were the locations where the Christians learned what it was they had embraced.

But by the time of the first apologists in the mid-second century, some Christian leaders had begun to realize that they needed a more extensive or more focused way to teach. After trying various philosophies, Justin Martyr became a Christian, learned much, and then set up shop in Rome to teach. He did not found a formal school, a place to study with a large archive and official ecclesial funding and support. It was by no means haphazard or only situational, but it was more of a popular level school where he received his students where he lived—or thereabouts—and taught not only the dedicated but also those who were passing through. He continued to wear the "philosopher's cloak" that identified him to others as a philosopher (as did some other Christians, such as Tertullian). He thereby made two claims that would have been obvious to those in Rome: first, that Christianity was a philosophy to be learned as one learns another philosophy such as Stoicism or Pythagoreanism, namely, by apprenticing oneself to a master; and, second, that he was a master qualified to teach that philosophy.

From his writings we can infer that Justin's education was substantial though not that of the philosophical top rung. But for him, as for other teachers who began to teach in Rome, the point was not to climb that ladder as much as it was to climb another—that of the transformation of the person by means of the truth revealed in Christ.[4] Justin taught, as did all early Christian teachers, that your knowledge and the shape of your life were one, unified thing. Where we tend to divide knowledge and life from each other, the ancients knew that you could only know as you live and that the knowledge that really matters most for your life is the knowledge of how to be in the world truly. Justin's school was a school that aimed to form Christians into Christians, to teach them who and what they were to become.

Rome was a place where Christian teaching was prevalent, as well as where various wayward theologies claiming Christian heritage came to roost (Marcion's, for example). But there were other cities, too, where Christians established education as an outworking of what their faith required. Alexandria in Egypt, to mention a prominent one, had long been a site of extensive pagan and Jewish philosophical reflection and archival collection. The early Christians participated in this legacy and simultaneously realized the need to build their own collection of texts and teach their specific way of life. As a young man at the turn of the second to third century, the great Origen not only studied under the Platonist Ammonius "the sack-wearer," he also spent time teaching at the first level of the traditional educational program ("grammar"). His familiarity with the classical way of training and with its associated content was extensive. But rather soon he began to teach more and more Christians and more and more Christian theology, and to compose some of his more famous works ("On First Principles," is one example).

Though past scholars have wondered exactly what the context was in Alexandria for Origen's Christian teaching, it now seems rather clear that Origen taught in a school at what Clemens Scholten calls the "collegiate level."[5] The Alexandrian Christians had opened a distinct institution, a novel form of education for instructing Christians in theological knowledge well beyond what catechumenates would have received and in counterpoint to the regular pagan course of study. This novel institution was what the church historian Eusebius later called "a catechetical school" (*HE,* 6.3.3). It was not yet a full-blown university in the way we conceive of universities from the Middle Ages onward, of course, but it was a remarkable invention that made the point: to educate Christians in a pagan world required the invention of Christian education.

For a variety of reasons, Origen eventually moved on to Caesarea-by-the-Sea in Palestine. It was there that he founded and developed the first true Christian university. In Caesarea Origen presupposed that his students had already progressed through the basic course of education. He taught at the highest level, shaped the philosophical curriculum to culminate in explicit theology, and attracted Christian students who became richly educated in advanced exegesis, hermeneutics, and allegory. The school also assembled archives that rivaled those of the Alexandrian church. Learning at the highest level, the Caesarean university realized, required regular access to the works that could generate research, reflection, and new insight.

Research was not "for its own sake," however, but was theologically grounded in the role of the institution in the overall sense of Christian life. The point was that the Christian mission to the world had a stake in university-level education. The students were not just anyone who happened to live in Caesarea or nearby, but those who could work at an advanced intellectual level for the sake of Christian truth.

Moreover, Origen was not an armchair thinker whose private life had no bearing on what he thought or taught. There was no such thing, in fact, as the modern conception of a private life. From his days in Alexandria, Origen's asceticism was inseparable from his teaching. He went barefoot and apparently had only one cloak. As Eusebius notes, with this practice Origen literally embodied the words of Jesus (*HE,* 6.3.10; Matt 10:10). (His early teacher Ammonius may also have influenced him, as asceticism was common to certain strands of philosophical life in antiquity.) As well as Origen could teach allegory, he also showed what literal exegesis entailed.

In Caesarea the students and teachers lived in close fellowship, and the students thus had ample time to observe their teachers and apprentice themselves to them. The school practiced the conviction that discipleship was the sort of knowledge at which Christians aimed. The highest of the heights of allegory were related to the way one ate, slept, spoke, dressed, and lived.

Inventing institutions—Christian schools of varying levels of education—would be rather pointless, of course, were the schools simply to teach what was already available in pagan culture. What, then, did they teach? Why did the early Christians think they needed to develop a specific sort of education?

In the context of the ancient world, the answer is completely audacious: the Christians began what can only be described as a "cultural takeover bid."[6] A tiny minority spread across the Mediterranean thought nothing less than, in contradistinction to their surrounding society, that they possessed the true words of life—and they thought that these words had to be taught. They thus replaced the foundational Homeric literature of the pagan curriculum with the Bible. They thereby begin to offer an alternative imagination for how to be in the world. It was a *scriptural* imagination. Such an imagination could not come simply by thinking or by any natural means; no one is born into the world with a scriptural imagination already in place. It, like being Christian itself, was something that had to be taught.

Christians, like Jews, were from the beginning a people of the book. Their need to teach interpretation of scripture was not only rooted in their Jewish heritage however, but, as they saw it, also in the explicit teaching of Jesus himself. At the end of Luke's Gospel, the resurrected Jesus twice gives exegetical lessons to his disciples. To Cleopas and his companion, Jesus interpreted "in all the scriptures the things concerning himself" (Luke 24:27). And later "to the Eleven and those who were with them," Jesus said "everything written about me in the law of Moses and the prophets and the psalms must be fulfilled." He then "opened their minds to understand the scriptures" and said, "thus it is written that the Christ should suffer and on the third day rise again from the dead and that repentance and forgiveness of sins should be preached in his name to all the nations, beginning from Jerusalem" (Luke 24:45).

In his resurrection appearances Jesus made the enduring point that to know who he is as Messiah is to read and search the scripture, and that to understand the mission of the church is to read and search the scripture. His resurrection has brought new creation, but to understand new creation is to return to scripture again and again. Every New Testament text bears witness in one way or another to the importance of scripture for articulating who Jesus is and what Christians are to be and do in light of him. Paul, for example, repeatedly teaches his churches to interpret their lives inside the scriptural story of God's dealings with Israel and the trajectory toward their own formation as Christ's body.[7] With its astonishing beginning—a rereading of the creation story in Genesis in light of the preexistent Word that is Jesus in the flesh—the Gospel of John teaches its readers to understand the whole of creation as the arena of the Word. All words can thus be brought into the service of this Word.

Early Christian education was thus a "conversion to a new sacred literacy in a new textual community."[8] The new literacy and new textual base did not mean that the early Christians forsook the knowledge they could gain from the classical/pagan world. Initially at least, most Christians who went to school still went to the lowest levels of school with their pagan neighbors and were trained in the typical course of study. Christian teachers, too, taught in the classical curriculum—as is evidenced by, among other things, Julian the Apostate's ban against them. Concurrently with such schooling, however, students were educated in church into the textual patterns of scripture as the context into which all other texts were to be fitted, and their classical curriculum was subordinated to a wider scriptural grammar: Julian was no fool; indeed, he banned Christian teachers because he saw things correctly. At the higher and highest levels of education, though the masters and students alike knew pagan philosophical texts, scripture was the text from which the Christians learned. Despite the survival of the old educational system, that is, the earliest Christians quite intentionally used the Bible to replace Homer—and Plato, and the rest—as the authoritative religious or philosophical texts; "the whole integrated literary and symbolic culture that surrounded them" was reinterpreted through the lens of scripture.[9]

No educated Christian thought, however, that scripture was superior to pagan literature by virtue of its style or beauty. Indeed, Christian apologists felt compelled to answer charges against them based on the rather homely nature of their texts when compared to elite pagan writings. The Christian claim about scripture was about content and effect. Study these words, they taught, and you will be transformed.

And that is ultimately the answer to *why* the early Christians developed institutions of education. They did not see education as the satisfaction of intellectual appetite but as the formation and transformation of teacher and student alike into the image of Christ. To learn was to become the community of the body of Christ and the human being as Jesus revealed it to be. They could not do this within the existing structures erected on the Homeric template and thus had to develop modes of learning that allowed them to reshape life in light of the truth of scripture. The effect of education was existential in the sense that it aimed to put Christians into the world who remembered who they were and knew that pursuing the truth meant, in Johannine terms, "doing the truth." It is a sobering and striking fact that the two early Christian teachers mentioned most in this chapter, Justin and Origen, both exhibited the unity between erudition and discipleship. Like their teacher Jesus, both Justin and Origen were killed for their witness to the truth.[10] In this way, they had become like the one whose Word they were trying to teach. And that is finally what it was for the early Christians to teach.

Care

Charities abound in our time. Indeed, they have become so much a part of the fabric of our culture that their existence is taken for granted. No one is surprised after a major hurricane, say, that Samaritan's Purse shows up on-site passing out water and food and helping to rebuild. No one is shocked when in the checkout line the clerk at the grocery store asks if you want to "round up" to help children with cancer. Charities have made it possible to help people near and far, even those whom we don't know and never will, with a click of the mouse or a "sure, I'll round up."

When we get really sick, most of us assume that we can go to the hospital and get care. Even if we know that insurance battles and bills are coming, we also know that if we're sick enough the hospital will not turn us away. In this country at least, we also assume that if there were a serious outbreak of contagious disease, the CDC and other major medical centers would at least attempt to mount a vigorous and systematic response. We also assume that there will be arenas of compassion: doctors, nurses, chaplains, pastors, and others who will tend to the sick.

In short, we assume structures of care, a vision of care, a reason for care. We have forgotten how such things came into the world in the first place, how they are not simply a given in human history, and how it was that the Christians generated the forerunners of the kind of care we now hope for—and why they did so.

In order to keep the Christian vision of the human alive and reveal it to the world, the early church created institutions that carried the view of the human in their practices and made it socially and politically visible. Understanding the Christian provision for the poor, the nursing during the plagues, the development of the hospital, and the invention of the orphanage is the same thing, that is, as seeing the concrete social and political explanation of the human revealed by God in Jesus Christ.

🯄🯄🯄🯄🯄

To state the obvious: there have always been poor people. What there has not always been is a distinct group called "the poor"—a group to whom we have obligations and who requires a more thoughtful systematic response and provision. The early Christians invented this category, enabling indigent people to be seen for the first time as those with whom we are bound up in the world.

What enabled the early Christians to see the poor was not a native altruism, as if early churches were miraculously filled with groups of kind or altruistic people (any reading of Paul's letters would immediately make this clear). Nor was it because the church consisted of early modern liberals who believed they had discovered human rights. It was instead, first, because Jesus had preached on this matter with clarity and force. As Luke portrays the sermon in the synagogue in Nazareth, Jesus activates God's declarations in the book of Isaiah and says, here they are at this moment, coming to life now in me. That which is the heart of God as revealed in Isaiah stands before you now: "The Spirit of the Lord is upon me," he announces, "because he has anointed me to proclaim good news to the poor" (Luke 4:18/Isa 61:1). And then later, as he preaches in front of a great crowd, Jesus declares quite bluntly to his disciples: "Blessed are the poor," he says, "because *yours* is the Kingdom of God" (Luke 6:20—*yours* not *theirs*; he is talking directly to them). Second, it was because the early Christians had learned from the story of everything that the human being was the place to see Christ himself and to serve him. To serve their Lord was not only to obey his teaching but was also to be in the world with him as he showed up in the face of concrete human beings; the crucifixion taught them that the suffering, naked, and vulnerable human was indeed Christ.

The earliest Christians understood very quickly, that is, that the indigent were also Christ and that to serve him among them was to provide for them. The story of Acts begins with the church sharing all things in common and narrates the spread of the gospel as inseparable from the tending of the poor. And Paul, when commenting on what the leaders of the Jerusalem church asked of him, mentions only one major thing: that he remember the poor (Gal 2). Which he did; his letters and Acts show his constant work to tend to the churches most struggling with lack and to bring offerings to Jerusalem (Rom 15:26; Gal 2:10; 1 Cor 16:1; 2 Cor 8:4, 14-15; 9:1-12). So, too, the book of James is, among other things, a blistering attack on any and all Christians who divide matters of the spirit/soul from those of the body: "If a brother or sister is without clothes and lacks daily food, and if one of you says to them, 'Go in peace; be warm and be filled,' and yet you do not give them the necessary things for the body, what good is *that*?" (2:15-16).

The Jews, of course, had long attempted to bring relief to other Jews who needed it. The Torah was explicit about doing something to provide for other Jews who were lacking, and even spoke of the practice of "jubilee," where debts were canceled and new economic beginnings made possible (Lev 25f.). The Christians inherited this sense from scripture and then radicalized it.

They first provided for their own, as many of the early texts after Acts amply demonstrate. Despite the tendency of modern scholars to see Acts's economic pattern for community as "idealized," it was apparently taken seriously by the early Christians (Tertullian, *Apol.* 39; *Apostolic Constitutions*, 2.26 et passim). The earliest apologist, Aristides of Athens, even claims that if there are poor Christians within a community whose own resources are limited, the community members "will fast two or three days that they might supply the needy with their necessary food" (*Apol.* 15). Churches kept lists of widows who needed goods, wrote to other churches about the support they provided, and even gave specific instructions on what to give to whom ("a coat to Sophia," for example, as one papyrus tells us). Indeed, Christian provision was extensive and public enough that it became known early in the second century to culturally observant pagans such as Lucian, who mocks the Christians for their gullibility: The huckster Peregrinus had pretended to be a Christian and was then imprisoned. While in prison and in need, so Lucian tells it, Peregrinus was ministered to by the naive Christians, who gave freely from what they shared in common.

Over time, the radical commitment to see Christ's face and blessing in the poor meant that the Christians also began to provide for those outside the fold. This move, as Peter Brown puts it, was a genuinely "new departure" in the ancient world and "threw open the horizons of society."[11]

Prior to the Christian intervention, there were no Roman programs of poverty relief. There were, of course, various attempts to halt famines with influxes of free or low-cost food, but all such provisions were tied to citizenship. Assuming they could produce evidence of their citizenship, for example, rich and poor received the same amount of grain. In the eyes of the Romans, it was the cities that needed the help, not the poor within them. The emperors and the mighty were benefactors of the cities and their citizens. City and citizen, citizen and city—that was the bond that really counted and the way society was seen.

The Christians, however, looked on those in society with profound need and for the first time in the Roman world saw not cities and citizens but the *poor*. This move created a new social imagination and linked people together in one complex whole. The Christians, that is, conceptualized the social fabric in a way that tied all humans together with respect to their economic vulnerability or lack thereof—whether in cities or countryside, it did not matter. The destitute were the poor. No longer was *citizen* elevated above economic reality; *poor* now received priority. Indeed, so much so that the Christian bishops became known as the "lovers of the poor."

As the communities of Christians grew, and then exploded, around the Mediterranean, it became clear that they needed to use ecclesial structure to ensure that the distribution of goods continued. Both before and after Constantine the bishops were responsible for keeping alive the Christian practice of loving the poor. Having created the category of persons to whom the church was to minister, over many years of practice the bishops "soaked significant areas of late antique society in the novel and distinctive dye of a notion of 'love of the poor.'"[12]

By the fourth century, one of the most important ways the love of the poor was instilled in the working understanding of Roman society was through the Christian invention of the shelter for the poor (the *xenodocheion*). Such places were (frequently) distinct buildings that functioned in a variety of ways to protect and serve the poor—including the wandering poor and refugees, who were on the move in search of better things. Indeed, by ministering to the poor on the move, the Christians made visible a hitherto "invisible class of migrants, to whose movements no one had paid much attention before."[13] They even served lepers, sometimes to the chagrin of the local populace, as when the bishop John Chrysostom erected the shelter for lepers in close proximity to a respected area in Constantinople. The *xenodocheia* were in all likelihood what captured the emperor Julian the Apostate's attention and imagination, and what he had in mind when he wrote to the pagan priest Arsacius in Galatia: the

Christians, said Julian in his letter, provide not only for their poor but also for ours.[14]

Along with the bishops' role in distributing goods to the poor, such institutions became the backbone of the church's eventual tax-exempt privilege. So long as the church provided for the poor, it was sheltered from imperial taxes. This combination of caring for the indigent and receiving tax benefits elevated the church's ministry to the poor into a work of civic goodness. For the first time in the history of the West, the poor were a focus of a charitable program as a feature of the way wider society was conceived and lived. The Christians had created a public virtue.[15]

In short, the Christian vision of the human was put to work through ecclesial structure and the creation of institutions. The earliest Christians had learned to see the poor and then practiced this knowledge, which in turn made them visible as "the poor" for the first time in Roman history. As the example of the lepers intimates, the Christians had also learned to see the sick. To that we now turn.

The sick, like the poor, have always been around. From all the "magical" papyri that have been recovered from the Egyptian desert, spells for health stand out as one of the two most basic types (spells for love, as I mentioned earlier, is the other). The sick flocked to pagan temples associated with the gods of health (Asclepius chief among them), to magicians, and to physicians if ever possible. They tried home remedies, and went without anything resembling health care at all. There was simply no organized, community-wide health care in the Roman world.

There were doctors of course, and many of them were as deeply educated in their knowledge and art as today's doctors are in ours. But typical medical care by trained physicians took place in private homes rather than in clinics or hospitals, which were nonexistent. The wealthy and those near the upper the end of the economic spectrum were the ones who received private physician care and who could avoid the quacks.

Some historians of medicine have thought that the early Christians systematically avoided regular medicine in favor of prayer and miraculous cure. There were perhaps a few Christians here and there who thought this way, but as a whole the Christians, like anyone else, believed in the "natural" causes of diseases and their natural treatment. They also believed in demons and the need for exorcism, but careful study shows that by and large they differentiated these special cases rather clearly from the manifold sorts of illnesses that required basic care.[16] From the start, the earliest Christians emphasized that the "salvation" they preached was not simply for the soul. Indeed, they did not believe in a body/soul dichotomy in the first place. Even remarkable healings could be described as "salvation" in the plain physical sense of remedy: sight to blind, for example (Luke 18:42; Acts 4:9). As they saw the poor, so they saw the sick: fully embodied, fleshly fellow-humans who figured forth the image of the King and who were thus to be honored, adored, and loved as they loved their King.

Perhaps nowhere was the Christian vision of the sick human as Christ on more prominent display than during a plague. All the records show that plagues were absolutely terrifying experiences for the people who experienced them. They decimated armies, cities, villages, anything in their path. Thucydides spoke once for all when he wrote about a plague in Athens well before Roman times. Doctors were useless, he said, and the people were afraid to visit one another. They thus "died with no one to look after them; indeed there were many houses in which all the inhabitants perished through lack of any attention . . . the bodies of the dying were heaped upon one another, and half-dead creatures could be seen staggering about in the streets or flocking around the fountains in their desire for water. The temples . . . were full of the dead bodies of people who died within them . . . the catastrophe was so overwhelming that that people became indifferent to every rule of religion or law. . . . No fear of god or law or a human being had a restraining influence. As for the gods, it seem to be the same whether one worshipped them or not" (*Hist. Pelop. War*, II.vii.). Whenever we find comments about the effect of plagues, they echo Thucydides's description and sentiment. The plagues were a horror.

The early Christians faced two devastating plagues, the so-called Antonine Plague beginning in A.D. 165 and the second plague about a century later (c. 250–60). Against all common sense and the practice of the

73

time, the Christians saw the plagues as an opportunity. Where even the celebrated physician Galen fled Rome to his villa in Asia during the first of these plagues, the Christians thought here was their chance, writ large, to show how they discerned Christ in the sick and nursed them accordingly. In Alexandria during the second plague, the Christian bishop Dionysius reported that in the attempt to avoid the plague, the pagans "would thrust away even those who were just beginning to become diseased," and that they "fled from their loved ones. They would even cast them out in the roads half-dead and treat the unburied corpses as vile refuse." The Christians, by contrast, "visited the sick unprotected, assiduously serving them, tending them in Christ" (letter cited in Eusebius, *HE*, 7.22).

Tending the sick did not mean that the Christians were impervious to the plague. Their nursing did not depend upon an assumption (or superstition) that they would avoid contracting the disease. Far from it; in fact, many did contract the plague, and many died. Those who served the sick, Dionysius wrote, were often "infected with the disease from others, drawing upon themselves the sickness from the neighbors, and willingly taking over their pains. And many, when they had cared for and restored to health others, died themselves, thus transferring their death to themselves." "In this manner," he continues, "the best of our brothers departed this life" (*HE*, 7.22).

Nor was this easy for them. Romanticizing is nowhere in the picture. Dionysius's contemporary in Carthage, bishop Cyprian, for example, wrote that "we are learning not to fear death." And those who died were clearly missed and longed for, as Cyprian put it, trying to comfort his people: those who have died "should not be mourned since we know that they are not lost but sent before, that in departing they led the way, that as travelers, as voyagers are wont to be, they should be longed for, not lamented" (*Mortality*, 15ff.). We might want to argue some with Cyprian about not mourning—lament, at any rate, is a foundational feature of biblical life—but his point should not be missed. The story that has put the Christians into the world as those who care for the sick is the same story that trains them not to fear death because it will not finally win. The absence of loved ones and friends is only momentary. Christ is in the sick, *important!*

the dying, the dead: this is the reality of crucifixion. But he is also on the other side of death, giving life and sustaining those whom we long for, ready to rescue us, too, as he did them, when we die.

Christian nursing practice also had a powerful effect on survival rates. When you are critically ill, there is a huge difference in your chances of survival between, on the one hand, being given something to drink, being cleaned, and being nursed, and, on the other, being thrown out into the road or left alone in your squalor at home. The survival rates doubtless contributed to the increase in the number of Christians in the empire not only because the Christians would have nursed one another well and thus survived better but also because the non-Christians who were nursed by Christians were more likely to join them after the plague passed. Many of these survivors would have lost key family members, or all of them, and would have found new loving brothers and sisters a good way to rebuild the social and relational bonds that make for life.[17] Moreover, Christian care made a profound impression on the survivors in the face of the norm of neglect. Yet, for the Christians themselves, growth was not the point or reason for action. The point was, rather, that the plague-infested human being was no less Christ than the healthy one and thus was exactly the person who needed care. Fear of death and even death itself were not to get in the way; life would win in the end.

Thankfully, plagues were not the normal way of things. But sickness was. Of the professions and trades Christians entered in the early centuries for which we have explicit record, physicians outnumber them all. Moving from the first to the fifth centuries, in fact, follows an upward curve: Treating the ill proved more and more attractive to Christians as the Christian view of the human took root. Such doctoring, however, was a far cry from mirroring the cultural practice of treating only the well-to-do in their homes. To the contrary, monastic infirmaries were the first to become places of care, and the birth of the hospital followed shortly thereafter.

Hospitals are so much a part of the modern landscape that we too easily forget that they had to be invented. They did not simply grow out of the ground as a natural response to illness. "The hospital was, in origin and conception, a distinctively Christian institution."[18] In the middle of the fourth century, the most famous and likely the first major hospital was developed on the outskirts of Caesarea by Basil the Great. The Basileias, as it came to be called after him, was a creative, multipurpose institution of care: The poor, the destitute, the homeless, orphans, and lepers, among others, were all served within different sections of the "new city," as his friend Gregory Nazianzen called it. Trained physicians and nurses lived there, and patients were given a bed, shelter, nourishment, and treatment. They could also stay for as long as their treatment required—and at no cost to them. The institution was supported by the church and by the government, especially in the form of tax exemption. As Basil argued to the provincial governor, the hospital provided a crucial public service, not just for the poor but for the ill; consequently, it should be supported by the government. Much like love for the poor, therefore, the early Christian invention of the hospital created a public virtue and an institution that were theretofore nonexistent: systematic and comprehensive medical care for the sick. As Nazianzen said, with special reference to lepers, "no longer do we have to look on the fearful and pitiable sight of men like corpses before death, with the greater part of their limbs dead, driven from cities, from dwellings, from public places, from water courses. . . . Basil persuaded those are who are human beings not to scorn human beings, nor to dishonor Christ . . . by their inhumanity toward human beings" (*Oration*, 43–63).

Subsequent to the Basileias, hospitals around the eastern part of the Mediterranean expanded quickly; they eventually grew in the West as well. In all cases, they were Christian inventions. The long tradition of provision within and between churches paved the way for the innovative, institutional response to the truth of the human as Christians knew it to be. Absent the hospital, the Christian vision of the human in the sick had yet to make its way categorically into the world. By contrast, the creation of the hospital brought to life in tangible and taking-up-space-in-the-world ways what it was to see the image of God.

✶✶✶✶✶✶

Of the vulnerable people in the ancient world, orphans ranked near the bottom. In terms of the ability to influence life around them, they ranked near the bottom. In terms of their worth to society, they ranked near the bottom. Though some of the older Greek cities made provisions for orphans of fallen soldiers, by the time of the Roman Empire, no legal or systematic provision was in place for war-casualty orphans beyond that of the regulation of their potential guardians. For orphans who were not made so by the death of their fathers on the battlefield, there was nothing.

It is therefore quite striking that the scriptures of Israel unambiguously portray God as the protector of orphans, the one from whom they can seek help and who makes sure they are treated justly (Exod, Deut, Isa, Psalms, Prov, et passim). From start to finish, orphans are included among the weak who require care. And when the biblical texts need to speak of a *very* wicked person, they speak of someone who wrongs or even murders orphans (Isa; Jer; Ezek; Zech; Malachi; Psalms; Job, et passim). Though there were some practices in place for doing what God's law said to do, and though there were even acts of unusual generosity—the Maccabees gave their war spoils to the orphans and kept funds for them in the Temple, for example (2 Macc)—by and large the care for orphans still depended on immediate family members.

Orphans were frequently paired with widows. In fact, in the ancient world an orphan originally meant someone whose father had died; an orphan was fatherless, the mother a widow, both vulnerable without the father/husband. In the New Testament, it is once again the Epistle of James that ties provision for the vulnerable to true piety: "pure and undefiled worship in the sight of God is this: to visit the orphans and widows in their affliction and to keep oneself unstained by the world" (1:27). Something like James's point is also assumed by Ignatius and the author of *Barnabas*. The former characterizes his adversaries in Smyrna as those who neglect the orphan (Ign. *Smyrn.* 6.2) and the latter depicts those in the way of darkness as people who have no care for the orphan (Barn. 20.2). The apologist Aristides says that Christians deliver orphans from those who oppress them; Justin Martyr tells of community goods being used to support orphans; and Tertullian claims that the church uses its funds to bury the poor, provide for the elderly shut-ins, and support orphans, both boys and girls who have no means (Arist., *Apol.* 15; Justin, *1 Apol.* 67; Tertullian, *Apol.* 39). Most dramatic, perhaps, is the argument of Lactantius in the fourth century, who contended that worrying about the fate of one's children is no reason to avoid martyrdom. Christian martyrs, said Lactantius, can count on the fact that their children will be adopted by their brothers and sisters in Christ (*Div. Inst.* 6.12). As John Fitzgerald notes, the martyrdom of Perpetua and Felicity illustrates from the third century a preexistent practical basis for Lactantius's argument: Felicity was martyred, but her infant was adopted by a Christian woman (a "sister").[19]

By the third century, Christians were clearly adopting orphans to raise (*Didascalia Apostolorum* 17). Orphans were also occasionally adopted in the pagan world, but it was almost exclusively done by relatives or "family friends." Christian reasoning, however, created a new category: the orphan as such. Orphans were not just orphans-of-family-or-close-friends but *orphans*. Their mere existence required a response. The church thus sought to raise them. By so doing it grew. But, again, as with its nursing practice, growth was not the point or the goal. Whether it grew or shrank, the church knew from its story that it had to tend the orphan as it would Christ.

Over time, the Christians realized the care for orphans needed a more systematic response. In the mid-fourth century, they thus established the first orphanage (*orphanotropheion*). It was an "utterly unique, truly sui generis institution in the ancient world."[20] As with the sick and the hospital, the orphans had been made categorically visible in the world by means of the institution created for their care.

Conclusion

Where many in today's world outright object to institutions and where they seem to believe that we can move through the world without them, the earliest Christians understood from their story that in order to be truly in the world as Christians they had to think institutionally. Their institutional creativity was indispensable to being Christian in the first place.

They learned from Israel's history and from Jesus himself that there is no such thing as communal flourishing without order, no such thing as order without hierarchy, and no such thing as hierarchy without problems. But the point was that the growing structure of the burgeoning church was the way to work through the inevitable problems to enable the life-giving evangel to continue its spread into the world. It was also to ensure the development of the concrete path by which the Christian communities communicated with one another, learned how to act in the face of persecution, received newly written materials, engaged in works of charity, provided pastoral care and oversight, and developed dozens of other things that went into what it was to be a new church in the first few centuries.

They also learned that to become the people of God whom they were called to be they had to learn how to become that people. Which is to say that they learned they needed to teach and to be taught—not simply in conversation here and conversation there but in actual serious education, in the interpretation of scripture, and in the overall effort to lay down deep imaginative structures that would empower them to read the world Christianly and to be in it as Christians. They could do this only by creating education that displayed the unity of thought and practice in the life of the Christian teachers and students. The early Christians thus developed a set of institutions that embedded scripture in the intellectual habits and life-shape of the Christians who led their communities in the stewarding and transmission of knowledge.

They also learned that the revelation of the true human required a creative and systematic response. They had to nurture the vision in intensely practical ways in order to bring it to life and broadcast it through Mediterranean society. To see others as Christ and to treat them in light of such a vision was a radical move in multiple dimensions. No one struggled to honor a king. But honoring Christ in the poor, the orphan, the leper, and the plague-infested was an entirely different matter. The vision of that kind of human as Christ was bound up with the realization that the human had a claim on Christian action toward it. And acting toward it, in turn, made a new vision possible in and for the world. The world now had space taken up by this new human and could now see—when it looked, for example, at Christian nursing practice or the Basileias—what Christians took the human being to be. The world saw "the poor" and the "orphan" for the first time. And it has never forgotten.

The importance of the early Christian institutions may seem obvious to us now. But that's only because we look at them retrospectively. Seen from the other side of history and set within the world in which they arose, they are nothing short of completely surprising. Why should God's truth be carried forward in an ecclesial structure that is obviously so fragile, so prone to disappointment and failure? Why should we educate people? Why should we start schools and universities that focus on the important things to learn? Why should we care for the poor? Why should we have hospitals? Why should we develop networks of adoption for orphans?

The critical point should now be clear. In order to keep the vision of the human alive, help it to develop staying power, and reveal it to the world, the Christians created institutions that both announced and stewarded their view of the human. To see how the church was thinking institutionally is to understand it as the concrete explanation of the human revealed by God in Jesus Christ. The witness to Christ, so the earliest Christians thought, required innovative structures that manifested the truth through their surprising existence in a world that had never seen them, did not anticipate them, and longed for them all the same.

Chapter 5
CONCLUSION

Christianity's entrance into the world was surprising. It brought things into the world that the world had never seen, and it created ways of seeing and being that have shone as the light of God down through the ages. Christianity was not without its hypocrites and its detractors, of course, but that it existed at all and that it grew into the most influential form of religious life in history is nothing short of absolutely stunning. The power of the gospel shaped a world.

After two millennia of existence, Christianity still has the power to surprise. It does so every day in the Global South and Far East, and it can do so even in the North Atlantic West, where we think we know what it is and have forgotten it at one and the same time. There is much at stake in recovering its power to surprise, and there are remarkable opportunities when we do. The power of the gospel can burst forth in surprising ways, bringing renewed life to established Christian communities, creating new ways of human healing and flourishing, and inviting the world to taste and see that the Lord is good.

The task of recovery is primarily bound up with (re)learning the story of everything and the view of the human being that it engenders. The overall work of Christian life will depend on the sense of the larger narrative we have and the human we see, even as that work will contribute to and reinforce the story and the vision of the human.

The work of recovering Christianity's surprise, however, is not only a work of (re)learning; it also requires the hard work of *un*learning. Foremost among the things we need to unlearn is the automatic and subconscious way we in the West have come to live a story that inculcates a view of the human that runs counter to a Christian vision of the human and is incapable of sustaining the social practices the human needs for a chance to remain—and become—what the Christians have given the world.

Relearning and unlearning the stories that make us who we are—that is the warp and woof of recovery of Christianity's surprise. We will take these in turn.

God and Not-God: The Story to Relearn

Since human identity is determined by the story or stories of which we're a part, what we need to learn and relearn most fundamentally is the story of everything and the commitments and practices that story gives us. That is how we will remember and relearn who we are and what we are to be doing in the world—and thus how we can once again be agents of Christianity's surprise. Since most of the book is already an unpacking of this story, we can be concise here at the end: The story of everything is the story of God and not-God, and there is nothing else. There is no wider story that encompasses that story. It is the one story within which all other stories can be told.

Of course, some people will tell you that we are no longer in a time of "metanarratives" or "just one" story that is the story of all things. Frequently their pronouncements will be accompanied by the assertion that comprehensive stories are inherently oppressive, smother all difference, and so on.

The truth, however, is that human beings don't need comprehensive stories to oppress other human beings. Sadly, we seem to have done this just fine from time immemorial and in every culture we've ever had. Nor do metanarratives smother difference simply by being meta, as some awareness of the vast differences in Christian life across the globe past and present would plainly show. Even more obvious, however, is the fact that the "no-metanarratives" narrative is itself a metanarrative about why we can't have metanarratives. It offers no reason for its claim to the universal truth that we should have no universal truth. Such self-contradiction is often unnoticed and made worse because it is frequently paired with self-righteous moralizing and historical ignorance. Under closer inspection, it turns out to be little more than a ham-fisted grab at power disguised as critique. Christianity has always had a story, and as long as there is anything Christian in the world, our story will be there, too.

The Christian claim from start to finish is that the story of everything is the narrative we have been given by God to redeem us from the things that would wound and destroy us both from without and from within. Christians do not claim to have invented or discovered this story but to have received it as the way they articulate what happened in the life, death, and resurrection of Jesus Christ. They also claim that the way to know who and what the human being is is to locate it within that story—and that to locate its identity somewhere else is to distort or pervert the understanding of what the human truly is. They also claim that the story of everything is lived as much as it is thought, that thinking and living are not to be divided, that the story implies certain kinds of practices and requires certain institutions, and that, in turn, these practices and institutions embody and broadcast the story itself. When Christians fail to embody the story and broadcast something that betrays it, hypocrisy becomes the character of the witness that testifies simultaneously *against* Christian betrayal and *for* the truth of the story itself. Exactly because Christians understand their betrayal as *betrayal* they know that their identities have been rightly formed by the story that tells them who they are and how they are to be in the world.

The earliest Christians believed that they had been swept up in this grand story of everything. It was within this narrative that they located their lives and from it that they derived their specific patterns of action for how to be in the world. Because everything that was not-God was God's, the Christians were interested in everything and, in principle, committed to everything that was not-God for the sake of God. No stone should be left unturned, no hidden recess left unexplored. Wherever God's light could possibly shine, there the Christians were to be.

In short, the early Christians attempted to live out the story that gave them their humanity—the shape of the lives in which they discovered who the human truly was. It set them free to proclaim the gospel anywhere and everywhere, to disobey the Roman demand to worship, to risk death in a plague, to care for each other in costly ways, to raise children who were not their own, to build hospitals, to establish places of rest for the indigent and homes for orphans, to take time to educate themselves in the reading of scripture, and to do all these things—and many, many more—without any obvious earthly reward. Freedom for them was freedom from self-obsession and self-protection and for obedience and service to Christ in every corner of the earth. And it was freedom to hope in and to anticipate God's good work everywhere even in the face of demise and death. The resurrection of Jesus established a future beyond death to which the Christians looked forward and which reached back into the midst of the present. Their vision was for eternity, and that gave them remarkable freedom and power in the present. They believed that life would win even when death struck its mortal blow. And they thus trained not to fear death in a world full of its obvious power. And *that* meant that no matter what came their way, the Christians were completely free to surprise the world. They had good news, and they were going to share it. High and low, near and far, the gospel went to work.

The Autonomous Individual: The Story to Unlearn

Since human identity is determined by the story or stories of which we're a part, what we need to *un*learn most fundamentally in our time is the prevailing story that runs counter to the story of everything. It is true that in some ways the late modern world is a time when we are awash in fragments of various stories and may, as a consequence, lead fragmented lives. It is also true, however, that there is a particular narrative about the human being and its possibilities that has long been dominant and continues to be so, even among all the fragments. It is the most destructive story for self-perception and human community that currently exists because it fundamentally recasts the human being as something it is not—and, as a result, eviscerates over time the possibility of life-giving and sustaining practices that go with the true vision of the human. We have to work hard to get free of it because it is almost impossible for modern Westerners—all of us—not to be caught up by its narrative. That story is the story of the autonomous individual.

In brief, the story of the autonomous individual says that the "I" is self-sovereign, emerges into the world without any prior obligations that have been placed upon it, and chooses the laws it has for itself. This story requires us to imagine an isolated individual, unconnected by any necessity to anything else at all and able to make for itself the life it chooses to make. The will of this individual is inherently free and chooses from an original position of freedom what sort of attachments and commitments it will have. Nothing can be forced upon the autonomous self from without that it does not agree to from within. When someone or something— a person, other people, various groups, governments, and so forth—tries to force the "I" to accept something it does not will to accept, the "I" is violated. The border between the "I" and the world of self-chosen obligations has been broken, and the invaders have entered territory that is not theirs. The territory of the "I" is mine alone—inviolable, sovereign, free.

The implications of the story of the autonomous individual are too numerous to unpack, for they are, in the end, intrinsically tied to the conditions that make the modern West in all its complexity. But there are four ways this story informs our basic understanding of the human and what we're up to in the world that we need to focus on so that we can unlearn them. Once again, we will be very brief so that we can get to the heart of the matter.

The first significant implication is for the way we come to know who we are. Or, more precisely, the way I come to know who I am. In the story of the autonomous individual, I learn who I am not as a gift from my Creator but by asking myself. I can ask others, too, if I like, but I am not bound to any of their opinions and can pick what I like from them and reject what I don't. Any claims about who I really am—religious, philosophical, relational, psychological, whatever—are true of me only to the extent that I recognize them as something I'm willing to say of myself. The final authority for my identity is myself. I determine who I am.[1]

The second significant implication is for the way we understand community. In the story of the autonomous individual, community is necessarily understood as a group of sovereign selves who agree for one reason or another to come together. These individuals are not bound by anything more fundamental than their own wills. Individuals can come and go "at will." The communities are, as they are now commonly called, "voluntary societies" (*voluntas* = will). Of course, the individuals may agree that their agreements are very important, and they may thus agree to form a "contract" of some kind, a sort of willing submission to a set of conditions for membership in a community. In the story of the autonomous individual, however, these conditions for membership could never be seen as binding truths about the human being's obligations or anything so grand. They are, and always will be, no more and no less than agreements based in the individual wills of the "I"s who choose to agree with one another.

The third significant implication is for the way we understand moral order. In the story of the autonomous individual, there are only two real universal moral commitments: first, of the self to itself, and, second, of all sovereign selves to the idea that no other sovereign self can impose itself in any way on any other. The violation of the sovereign self is immoral. Beyond that there is no binding moral structure, nothing to call to or compel the sovereign self apart from the agreement to be bound to other autonomous individuals. And that can be broken at will.

The lack of a binding moral grain beyond the autonomous self turns out to mean that all other "moral" claims are really nothing of the sort. They are simply expressions of ourselves—our desires, our preferences, our emotions, our likes and loves. We may feel very passionate about them, we may believe everyone else should see things as we do, but what we cannot do without destroying the story about ourselves as individuals is to claim that our predilections should be someone else's, too. Even if we say or do something that results in much agreement from other individuals, in the story of the autonomous individual our speech/action is no more than preference—an individual's self-projection into and onto the world for others to see. When there is agreement on an alleged moral issue, it is agreement between individual self-projections, not a discernment of the moral grain of the issue that reaches beyond the individuals to a truth irrespective of their opinions about it. No matter the issue on which agreement is reached, statements such as "It is right" or "It is wrong" when uttered by autonomous individuals can never mean more than "we agree that we like this" or "we agree that we do not like this." This is why current public discourse is so impoverished and discouraging: the attempt to "argue" others around to a particular position they do not want to take has become shrill and desperate, a kind of screeching or accusing or guilt-mongering, because we have ingested enough of the story of the autonomous individual to intuit that no amount of argument or attempted persuasion can really compel someone who does not want to be compelled. And so debate becomes something more like yelling. But our yelling amounts to only this: "you should like this, too!" Or "my tastes should be yours!" Or "I don't like what you like!" And so on and on in an unwinnable shouting match.

The fourth significant implication follows directly from the first three. It is the recourse to legal coercion, which, in the end, is always backed by force. Since there is nothing beyond individuals to hold them to certain standards they do not choose or to direct their behavior even against their wills and desires, there is nothing written into the way the world is that can create the conditions for life together. And since human beings always live life together in one way or another, and since most do not prefer complete anarchy, we have to force the conditions that make for life together. We cannot rely on other people to choose the things we'd prefer for them to choose; and they cannot rely on us to choose the things they'd prefer for us to choose. We can hope they do, and they can hope we do, and that's the most we can hope for. When our agreements somehow converge, and we get a contract, we thus have to make laws that will enforce the contract and keep some modicum of functional society. Lawyers have a central place in the story of the autonomous individual precisely because they must exist to enforce the contracts that we agree to but to which we are not truly bound. We have to force people to do what we know they don't really have to do as autonomous individuals.

As the story of the autonomous individual has gained influence over the years, the number and reach of the lawyers have also grown. The expansion of the legal profession and its (eventual or potential) reach into every area where humans have contracts is exactly what we should expect if autonomous individuals are going to live by the contracts they agree to create. Law, and the force that backs it, are conceived and used as resistance to the implosion of a society that believes the story of the autonomous individual. The lawyers are needed everywhere, that is, because the view of the human in this story requires there to be lawyers everywhere to have even a small chance at decently functioning social bonds.

By ending the four implications of the story of the autonomous individual with law and force, we come easily to the inherent difficulties that plague this story and the societies that arise from and with it. The reliance on law and force shows that what the story of the autonomous individual pushes out the front door comes racing in again through the back door: The story says that no one can be compelled against the will of the "I" to do something the "I" does not itself will, but the social results of this view require people to be compelled. You can't compel, says the story, but you must compel anyway.[2]

The point about compulsion takes us to the two deep and inexpungible contradictions in the story that says the human is an autonomous individual. First, strictly speaking the autonomous individual has no story that it does not will for itself to have. It has only the story that it chooses as its story. The contradiction, of course, is that the story about the autonomous individual is the story that is already accepted, a given within the understanding that the sovereign-self chooses its own story. The story of the kind of self that the self is is not chosen. It is the story that makes the sovereign-self appear to itself as self-sovereign in the first place. The story that the autonomous individual tells about itself is thus dependent on the acceptance of a prior story about what sort of self can fashion its own story. Autonomous individuals claim to have no givens but their entire picture is their given, namely, the story that there are no givens for the autonomous individual.

The second contradiction in the story of the autonomous individual is this: According to the story, if I am an autonomous individual and you are, too, I cannot impose anything upon you and you cannot impose anything upon me—except that I can impose on you the law that you cannot impose on me anything that I do not choose.

We can take something that was crucial to the early Christians as an example to illustrate the point, the care for the poor: You say I should care about the poor; I see no reason why I should care and take your insistence to be an imposition, an infringement of my freedom to choose what I care about. I then tell you to back off, leave me alone, and impose on you the necessity to stop imposing on me. If you in your self-autonomy decide that you reject my imposition and, in turn, try to impose on me the law that I cannot impose anything upon you, I can then reject your imposition on me and try again to impose upon you . . . and on it goes. Each imposition is a denial of the freedom the other autonomous individual has by rights inherent to being a sovereign self, and each rejection of each imposition is a rejection of the freedom of the other individual. Exactly because of its autonomy, the autonomous individual is in the end *necessarily* caught in a vicious cycle of imposition and rejection in relation to others. As long as there is more than one person in the world, and as long as these two or more people have to relate to each other in some way, the contradiction of "no-imposition" cannot actually be lived.

What these two contradictions mean is that the story of the autonomous individual cannot fund life together. It will break down and eventually fail, and the lives we've hoped to live together will come apart. (Indeed, we are witnessing the tremors of such failure now.[3]) But it is still the most powerful narrative about the human being that underpins much of the modern West. And it is both intoxicating and toxic to us all. It is intoxicating because there is a heady, even euphoric, sense of freedom that can come with the thought that I am truly able to determine my own life, that I am not bound to anything beyond myself and my preferences, that my obligations that weigh me down can be put aside, that I can decide who I am and what I want to be and do, and I can go my own way. But it is toxic because it promises me a way to love myself without God, and to live without his direction. And it finally leaves me all to myself, which is to say that I am left entirely alone.

The simplest reason Christians have to unlearn the story of the autonomous individual, therefore, is this: It makes the story of everything into a story about myself. "Everything" is finally drawn into the self that I take myself to be. Whatever is not of my-self is subject to myself. I am the ruler not only of myself but of all things in relation to myself. Which is to say that I have become God. The sovereignty that is proper to God is repositioned within the individual human. I am the God of my life, I am self-sufficient, I decide who I am, and nothing can intrude on my freedom to be exactly this self-ruled, self-sufficient, self-unto-itself. This is idolatry of the most basic kind: the inversion of the Imago. No longer does God image himself in me; I have taken God's image and turned myself into God. I am the God who images myself in the world.

Moreover, the story of the autonomous individual makes the human into a fundamentally anti-relational creature. I can of course choose to relate to anyone I choose, but at bottom the story of the autonomous individual makes any other self a potential threat to my self-autonomy simply by the fact that its existence necessarily posits an imposition upon me. You and I are locked in a perpetual imposition and are therefore most truly ourselves only when we are free of any imposition, that is, of each other. The flip side of this anti-relational self is tragic: I am abandoned. You are abandoned. And we cannot reach each other. We thus lose our common humanity in the attempt to be ourselves.

Taken together, the story that makes us God on the one hand and an isolated "I" on the other is a story that rejects the true God and the true human. When we live it, we have nothing with which to surprise the world. The world already knows—and knows all too well—what it's like to exalt yourself above all else, to ignore the existence of others or wish them to go away, to be abandoned, and to live without God.

Surprise

The early Christians could not imagine living without God. They believed that they had received the gift for the ages. And they believed that that gift was to be shared with everyone. To read the pages of the New Testament and the Christian literature immediately thereafter is to be immersed in a joy that knows laughter, delight, healing, transformation, and life are at the bottom of all things. The excitement that they had something to offer the world is palpable, and their willingness to be creative, to risk, to fail in trying, and to get up again is everywhere evident.

Because they expected God to work all over the world, they had no boundaries and no limits. And because they knew that God's human image was in every person, they invited everyone to come in, and tended even those who would not.

Very quickly they learned to think that no city and no neighborhood was too lost to be there, no Roman official was too powerful to reach, no poor drunkard was beyond help, no abandoned child should be left to fend for itself, no sick and helpless person should suffer and die alone. The Christians should be present in the world's pain, should be attentive to its needs, should work energetically for the truth of the gospel in practice, and should expect God to bear fruit from such faithfulness. The Christians thus had a confidence and a sense of anticipation wherever they went. They knew the gospel story and knew the power that it brought directly into the midst of human life. And they saw it at work in Jerusalem, Samaria, Antioch, Caesarea, Cyprus, Ephesus, Philippi, Lystra, Galatia, Thessalonica, Athens, Rome, Edessa, Dura-Europas, Alexandria, Spain, and beyond.

Their cultural footprint went from barely visible to massive in almost no time at all. They drew together people who otherwise had no reason to be together—or, indeed, had reasons *not* to be together—on the basis of a pervasive, structurally powerful identity and with creative communities and institutions that housed widely disparate people under a common roof. Their unity in Christ showed what the human was and made unlikely alliances across different and various divisions of life. In fact, the

Christians were a rather motley crew: Roman governors and peasants, sick and healthy, poor and rich, learned and ignorant, Jew and Gentile. All were being changed, all were being transformed.

No matter what someone did to make ends meet or what sort of political leanings they had or what kind of people they had been, the Christians aimed to build a family from among them: "brothers and sisters in Christ." This family was dispersed throughout the Mediterranean, but it was "one" through the tightly networked communication, leadership, and practice—sacramental, liturgical, and day-to-day—that persisted from Jerusalem to Rome and beyond. It was this unity that gave them their political ground and identity, and the ability to resist domination and the pressure to conform or dissolve. As individuals or as factions, they could neither have stood firm in the midst of the intense cultural forces that were against them nor grown so rapidly and effectively. They had fights among themselves, of course, which will occur anytime there is more than one person present, but to the outside world they were known by the name that unified them and fit their polychromatic look, their works, and their politics: Christians.

The earliest Christians met numerous obstacles. They knew rejection, persecution, and social stigmatization. They knew internal strife, defection, and lack of resources. But they were undaunted. Jesus told them it would be like this, and that at times they would even be lambs among wolves. He also told them that while being as innocent as doves, they would need to be as wise as serpents. So they tried to be wise. They planned how to structure their communities to get the most out of their growth, they thought hard about how best to resist cultural pressure to conform to things they could not accept, they cultivated a scriptural imagination, they taught "sound doctrine" to the faithful, they put down deep roots by building institutions that would last, and they connected the roots into one large ecosystem by a leadership structure, regular communication, extensive travel, and a shared mission.

In a word, the early Christians were a people of hope. They had witnessed the power of God over death, and they saw that power at work in the world through the formation of communities and institutions that both announced and embodied the gospel through their distinctive practices. They did not shrink from the hard truth of the world's recalcitrance; nor did they count on things turning out well simply because they bore the good news and tried to love the people whom God loved. Instead, they counted on the sure and certain hope that no matter how things turned out the power of God that was at work in raising Jesus from the dead was at work in their work. They were thus free to work with anyone and on anything that the gospel required.

If they needed to establish a call center in the middle of a Singapore prison to give the prisoners a taste of the gospel at work through the teaching of skills the prisoners would need on the outside, the early Christians would do so. If they needed to start a sanitation business in the middle of the slums in Indonesia or Kenya, the early Christians would do so. If they needed to welcome, provide safety and healing, and develop abilities for the future to women and children victimized and displaced by violence in Cambodia, Vietnam, and elsewhere, the early Christians would do so.[4]

If they saw an opportunity to repair lives wrecked by drugs, alcohol, and prison by teaching addicts how to build homes alongside Christian mentors who would work with them, the early Christians would jump on it. If they thought that gang members could be loved out of violence into a different way of life, they would love them. If they believed that they could change lives by teaching in the inner-city or impoverished rural areas, they would find teachers and teach. If they discerned that the legal arena was a fundamental place to establish and protect the human, they would develop and recruit talented lawyers and put them to work. If they saw that the teaching of law made all the difference for what lawyers became, they would create clerkships that allowed future professors to return to the law schools and get to work. If they figured out that judges were the hinge between law and its application, they would educate lawyers toward the wisdom they needed as judges and set them to work. If they saw that doctors were needed who had learned not to fear death and who were not in a hurry to go past the unfixable sick and vulnerable, they would train them and put them to work. If they learned that health care required people who could see the full human rather than treating a person as a machine with broken parts, they would establish programs to repair medicalized vision and put the participants to work.

If they realized that economists were needed who could think best about how to get the most out of the resources they had, they would enlist them and put them to work. If they believed that entrepreneurs and business experts were needed who could show how best to set up creative solutions to demanding problems, they would engage them and put them to work. If they saw a chance to keep alive the vision of the human by joining hands with Jews and other religious traditions in the face of practices that harm our humanity, they would reach out to them and join hands and work. If they discerned that they had more in common with Jews and other strong religious traditions in resisting the story of autonomous individuals than they did with reductive, secularized accounts of human identity, they would strengthen those ties and get to work. If they knew any people who sensed a genuine call to ministry in the church, they would rejoice, mentor them, and send them to be educated in the depths of the faith.

The earliest Christians' foundation for surprise was thus tied to a desire to be Christians above all else and the need to form and nourish Christian life, on the one hand, and, on the other, the desire to work with whomever and whatever they needed to work with to live out in the midst of the world the gift they had been given. The sense that I could live for myself and that, in the end, I am alone was nowhere to be found. To the contrary, the Christians believed that they were caught up in something dramatically larger than themselves, that they were bound to one another as family, that the world was hungry for what they had to give, that people would join them, and that all of them could be filled with the exciting work of a lifetime. They also believed—and this motivated them more than anything else—that they would be together when their lives were over and finally saw the Lord not only in his image but face to face.

Recovering this vision and the purpose and excitement that went with it will take time. There is no way to learn, or to unlearn, in a hurry. We will have to be patient, creative, and make the effort to go deep. We will, moreover, have to engage continually in the world and in patterns of Christian formation. The early Christians would teach us that becoming who we are as the image of Christ requires us to be in the world actively as that image and to develop modes of living that broadcast its implications for others.

That does not mean that we try to fix everything that is broken, that we rush into projects that promise positive outcomes. At first, in fact, being surprised once again may look more like slowing down in a world built on speed, sifting through the wealth of the tradition's wisdom, training our imaginations, and experimenting in a variety of contexts: with education, with ministry, with healthcare, with connections between a wide range of groups that have a stake in the vision of the human delivered by centuries of Christian conviction and practice. The surprise of Christianity is not that it offers instant solutions to society's perennial problems—as if it were primarily a grand social program with religious components—or that it can reverse the currents that move us away from its historical influence and somehow return us to a more "Christian" culture. The surprise is rather that Christians can bring good news in the midst of a vastly complicated world and live in ways that give us hope in the face of demise and death. That hope, in turn, generates the thought and practice that anticipates God's active, creative, and recreative work even among the disintegration of societal patterns—and that puts Christians in the world as a way the Lord's goodness can be tasted and seen.

In the end, Christianity's surprise is not an alternative theory in the face of secular accounts of the human or a quick action plan but an alternative way of life built on hope. It is ultimately because of our hope that—come what may—we can surprise the world with our witness to Christ in us and in every human who lives on the face of this earth.

NOTES

Chapter 1
INTRODUCTION

[1]Our context is now "pluralist," of course, but in the North Atlantic West, pluralism is a way of saying that there are other ways of being in the world on offer than Christianity. Christianity is still the dominant cultural backdrop to these alternatives, even to secularity. The rejection of religion in the North Atlantic West is not so much a rejection of an abstract concept ("religion") as it is a rejection of the history of influence of Christianity or of Christianity itself. Few Western secular intellectuals have really tried Hinduism, for example, or have it in their crosshairs. Nietzsche is an excellent example of the power of Christian influence in the West. He knew that when you want to reject God, the God you need to reject is the Christian God.

Chapter 2
THE STORY OF EVERYTHING

[1]Barbara Hardy, "Towards a Poetics of Fiction: An Approach through Narrative," *Novel* 2 (1968), 5, cited in Alasdair MacIntyre, *After Virtue* (3rd ed. South Bend: University of Notre Dame Press, 2007), 211–12.

[2]Matthew Novenson, *The Grammar of Messianism: An Ancient Jewish Political Idiom and Its Users* (New York: Oxford University Press, 2019).

[3]The Roman governor of Judea normally resided in Caesarea Maritima on the coast. In Jerusalem a small number of troops was regularly garrisoned in the fortress Antonia adjacent to the Temple. But at the pilgrimage festivals, the Roman brass and more military personnel were in town to make sure all went well.

[4]Many readers too quickly pass by the violence here and assume Peter was trying to cut off the ear. But thinking for a second about how you swing a sword should clear up the picture. If you swing down and get the ear vertically, you cut into and possibly through the collarbone area and the shoulder, and so on. Peter is swinging horizontally—a head chop—and Malchus leans his head to the side just in time to avoid decapitation. Peter gets his ear rather than his entire head.

[5]Barabbas and others were convicted of stasis—and the violence that goes with it ("murder")—and thus scheduled for execution.

[6]The irony here could hardly be thicker: he is of course King, and precisely through the crucifixion does he save.

[7]Acts 2:36 is often misread, even by professional New Testament scholars. In context, it does not mean "God made Jesus something he was not yet" but instead "God confirmed him as that which he always was." See my article "Acts 2.36 and the Continuity of Lukan Christology," *New Testament Studies* 53, no. 1 (January 2007): 37–56.

[8]Jews, of course, did think polytheism was false (idolatry). But they did not engage in mission and direct confrontation with polytheistic life—the active, coordinated attempt to convert any and all non-Jews away from their gods to the one true God, the God of Israel—in anything like the way the Christians did. As the New Testament illustrates, the Christians did just this from the beginning.

[9]Cited in Manfred Clauss, *Kaiser und Gott: Herrscherkult im römischen Reich* (Munich: K. G. Saur, 2001), 6.

Chapter 3
THE HUMAN

[1]Recapitulated simply means starting from the head all over again (*caput* is Latin for head).

[2]In the first century AD relations between Jews and Samaritans were poor. Samaritans were considered by Jews in Judaea and Galilee to be "half-Jews," which rather than increasing liking for one another actually increased dislike. After the Babylonian exile when the Jews begin to rebuild the temple, the Samaritans decided they would build their own temple. By Jesus's time it had been destroyed (built 332 BC and destroyed two hundred years later), but the memory of it was quite alive (it was rebuilt after AD 135 and destroyed for good in 484). In short, the Samaritans were considered to be another religious and ethnic group, one to which Jews were hostile (it was returned) and for which they had intense disliking. In fact, if we are to believe Josephus, for pilgrimage festivals, Jews from Galilee frequently traveled around Samaria to Jerusalem. On the significance of the Samaritan temple for early Christianity/Judaism, see the discussion in Timothy Wardle, *The Jerusalem Temple and Early Christian Identity* (Tübingen: Mohr Siebeck, 2010).

[3]This remaking entails the recognition that even as it continues to groan, all creation is to be reconciled to God (Rom 8; Col 1). And this recognition brings with it the opportunity and responsibility to care for all creation in ways that reflect God's reconciling work. That is, in biblical perspective the human being is alone the image of God, but imaging God

does not lead to a posture of detachment from the rest of creation—as if we could Lord it over all the world—but instead requires us to care for all of God's works.

[4]Martin Kähler, *The So-Called Historical Jesus and the Historic, Biblical Christ* (Philadelphia: Fortress Press, 1964), 80n11.

[5]Julian, Ep. 22, *Letter to Arsacius.*

Chapter 4

INSTITUTIONS

[1]"Jésus annonçait le royaume, et c'est l'Église qui est venue" (Alfred Loisy, *L'Évangile et L'Église* [Paris: A Picard et fils, 1902], 111).

[2]Hugh Heclo provides a helpful example to show thinking institutionally at work: If your house were to catch on fire and you had time to grab only one item, and you quickly grabbed the TV set as your only item to save, you would not be thinking institutionally. If, however, you grabbed your family album, you would be. See his *On Thinking Institutionally* (New York: Oxford University Press, 2011), 85.

[3]Robert L. Wilken, *The First Thousand Years: A Global History of Christianity* (New Haven: Yale University Press, 2012), 356.

[4]See Gustave Bardy, "Les écoles romains au second siècle," *Revue d'Histoire Ecclésiastique* 28, no. 2 (July 1932): 501–32.

[5]Clemens Scholten, "Die alexandrinische Katechetenschule," *Jahrbuch für Antike und Christentum* 38 (1995): 16–37.

[6]Frances M. Young, *Biblical Exegesis and the Formation of Christian Culture* (Cambridge: Cambridge University Press, 1997), 51.

[7]See Richard B. Hays, *The Conversion of the Imagination: Paul as Interpreter of Israel's Scriptures* (Grand Rapids: Eerdmans, 2005).

[8]Robin Lane Fox, "Literacy and Power in Early Christianity," in *Literacy and Power in the Ancient World*, ed. Alan K. Bowman and Greg Woolf (Cambridge: Cambridge University Press, 1994), 128.

[9]Young, *Biblical Exegesis and the Formation of Christian Culture*, 75, 79; cf. Arthur J. Droge, *Homer or Moses? Early Christian Interpretations of the History of Culture* (Tübingen: Mohr Siebeck, 1989).

[10]Justin was directly martyred; Origen was tortured until he was broken and died from his brokenness—both were like Christ.

[11]Peter Brown, *Poverty and Leadership in the Later Roman Empire* (Boston: Brandeis University Press, 2001), 6.

[12]Brown, *Poverty and Leadership in the Later Roman Empire*, 9.

[13]Brown, *Poverty and Leadership in the Later Roman Empire*, 32.

[14]Julian, *Ep.* 22.

[15]There were many changes throughout the Middle Ages to *xenodocheia* and so forth but, still, this was the basic dynamic that eventually led to charities as we know them and expect them to behave; the trouble is that by putting things in terms of civic goodness the church can forget its responsibility and turn it over to the government (the government is supposed to provide for the poor), which if history is any indication, is an ineffective and even harmful way to go.

[16]See Gary B. Ferngren, *Medicine and Healthcare in Early Christianity* (Baltimore: Johns Hopkins University Press, 2012).

[17]Rodney Stark, *The Rise of Christianity* (Princeton: Princeton University Press, 1996), chap. 4.

[18]Ferngren, *Medicine and Healthcare in Early Christianity*, 124.

[19]John T. Fitzgerald, "Orphans in Mediterranean Antiquity and Early Christianity," in *Perspectives on the Socially Disadvantaged*, ed. D. F. Tolmie, *Acta Theologica Supplement Series* 23 (2016): 29–48.

[20]Fitzgerald, "Orphans in Mediterranean Antiquity and Early Christianity," 44.

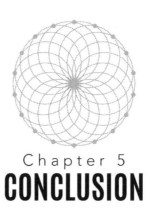

Chapter 5
CONCLUSION

[1]Someone might want to object that the "I" determines itself in light of certain natural givens. But in the story of the autonomous individual the "I" is under no obligation to these alleged natural givens and can decide which of the things that appear natural to other people are worth keeping and which aren't. "Nature made me this way"—shy, happy, whatever—is always subject to "but I choose instead to be. . . ."

[2]Our court system is jammed and backlogged not because there are morally crucial cases stacked one on top of the other but because legal recourse is all we have to compel other people to do something we want them to do in a society of autonomous individuals.

[3]Liberalism—the philosophy erected on this anthropological basis—is doomed to fail. We are witnessing its failure now as the various "I"s and "I"-groups destroy the common bonds we've long shared. Some think this is a time for radical retreat (Alasdair MacIntyre/Benedict Option), but as a whole the early Christians seemed much more invested in bringing Christ to the world. Other contemporary thinkers believe that we can still forge a common life by agreeing that we agree on some important things and simply going forward (Jeffrey Stout). But this second option is naive precisely because it ignores the inescapable role and place of force in the agreements (eventually one has to force people to agree with things in their behavior that they might not agree with in their hearts/minds/etc.). Christians are not wedded to any particular philosophy and are free

to move wisely in the world so long as we do so as Christians—and take whatever consequences come our way.

⁴Examples from Kim Tan and Brian Griffiths, *Social Impact Investing: New Agenda in Fighting Poverty* (London: Transformational Business Network, 2016). Many of the examples Tan and Griffiths offer exhibit precisely the kind of "risk" that the early Christians knew how to take.